CITYSPOTS
GDANSK

WHAT'S IN YOUR GUIDEBOOK?

Independent authors Impartial up-to-date information from our travel experts who meticulously source local knowledge.

Experience Thomas Cook's 165 years in the travel industry and guidebook publishing enriches every word with expertise you can trust.

Travel know-how Contributions by thousands of staff around the globe, each one living and breathing travel.

Editors Travel-publishing professionals, pulling everything together to craft a perfect blend of words, pictures, maps and design.

You, the traveller We deliver a practical, no-nonsense approach to information, geared to how you really use it.

CITYSPOTS
GDANSK
Marc Di Duca

Thomas Cook

Written by Marc Di Duca
Original photography by Marc Di Duca
Front cover photography (Old Town Square) © Peter Adams/www.photolibrary.com
Series design based on an original concept by Studio 183 Limited

Produced by Cambridge Publishing Management Limited
Project Editor: Ross Hilton
Layout: Paul Queripel
Maps: PC Graphics
Transport map: © Communicarta Limited

Published by Thomas Cook Publishing
A division of Thomas Cook Tour Operations Limited
Company Registration No. 1450464 England
PO Box 227, Unit 18, Coningsby Road
Peterborough PE3 8SB, United Kingdom
email: books@thomascook.com
www.thomascookpublishing.com
+ 44 (0) 1733 416477
ISBN: 978-1-84157-626-8

First edition © 2007 Thomas Cook Publishing
Text © 2007 Thomas Cook Publishing
Maps © 2007 Thomas Cook Publishing
Series/Project Editor: Kelly Anne Pipes
Production/DTP: Steven Collins

Printed and bound in Spain by GraphyCems

CONTENTS

CITYSPOTS

SYMBOLS KEY

The following symbols are used throughout this book:

ⓐ address   ☏ telephone   🖷 fax   ⓦ website address   ⓔ email
🕒 opening times   ⓝ public transport connections   ❶ important

The following symbols are used on the maps:

🛈	information office	○	city
🛫	airport	Ο	large town
➕	hospital	○	small town
🛡	police station	═	motorway
🚌	bus station	▬	main road
🚆	railway station		minor road
✝	cathedral	—	railway
❶	numbers denote featured cafés & restaurants		

Hotels and restaurants are graded by approximate price
as follows:

£ budget   ££ mid-range   £££ expensive

⏵ *Gdansk's Old Town by night*

INTRODUCING
Gdansk

Introduction

Look at a map of Europe and the Polish port city of Gdansk may not immediately leap out at you as a hip and exciting city break destination. Certainly, before arriving in Gdansk, most people's associations with the city will be of rusting shipyards, striking workers and the chilly, fog-bound Baltic. While some of the Eastern Bloc grit remains, the *Trójmiasto* (Tri-City) conurbation, comprising Gdansk, the resort of Sopot and the town of Gdynia, has scrubbed up rather well. You could say the area has it all – superb white sandy beaches lining the Baltic, historical sights stretching from its medieval heyday to the more recent days of Solidarity, a shockingly full-on nightlife scene, laid-back street cafés and highbrow culture in the form of the Opera House and classical music concerts. Thanks to the city's location on the Bay of Gdansk, water sports are big, and if kayaking and windsurfing appeal to you, this is the place to come. All in all, Gdansk, like many other destinations in the former communist bloc, is throwing off its stale, drab image and attracting a young crowd looking for excitement as well as some great places to chill out.

Gdansk is easily accessible by air from the UK and other cities around Europe. On arrival, a cheap and efficient public transport system means getting around the Tri-City is simple. Budget-conscious travellers will love the city, as restaurants, transport and accommodation remain cheap while standards are high enough. The kids will adore Sopot beach in summer, and couples can enjoy the romantic atmosphere of Gdansk's historical centre even during winter. The *Trójmiasto* really does have something for everyone, so for a cracking break in Poland, leave Warsaw and Kraków for next time, and come to the Baltic coast – you won't regret it!

🔺 *The historic Gdansk crane and waterfront*

When to go

CLIMATE

Unlike many European cities, which change unrecognisably over the summer months as locals abandon their city to hordes of tourists, July and August are by far the best months to visit Gdansk and the wider Tri-City area. In fact, cultural and social life migrates from Warsaw and other bigger cities over the summer as people escape the sweltering temperatures on the central plain and head for the cooler coast. The cold Baltic wind takes a break, the sun shines, the beaches are full of life and this is the time the area holds its best events. The street cafés are in full swing and beach parties in Sopot guarantee round-the-clock fun. The downsides to this, of course, are the tourist-choked streets, fully booked hotels and sky-high prices. Summer also sees by far the most rainfall and the most violent thunderstorms, but these never last too long. Expect temperatures in the low 20°sC (60°sF).

Those less concerned about getting a tan or beach-partying to the small hours may find spring and autumn pleasant seasons in the Tri-City. Temperatures are comfortable, there are fewer tourists and a trip out to Malbork or Hel can be a colourful experience as the countryside blossoms in spring or soothes the senses with the 'golden Polish autumn'. Autumn in central and Eastern Europe is perhaps the best season of all – the days are still long, it rains less and life reverts back to its normal course with students hurrying to lectures, farmers bringing in the last of the crops in the hazy light, schoolchildren heading to music lessons or walking obediently in file behind a

⬤ *The frozen banks of the Motława River in winter*

teacher and the bustle of the city giving an idea of what ordinary life is like in this part of the world.

Though Sopot closes down over the harsh Baltic winter, Gdansk is very much a year-round destination. Thanks to direct flights from the UK, increasing numbers of visitors are coming in what is normally regarded as the low season. Winter in Gdansk's Main Town with snow on the ground and a crisp chill in the air can be an atmospheric time, and Christmas and New Year take you back to a more traditional and romantic period. Be warned though, the wind will chill you to the core, so get those woollies out.

ANNUAL EVENTS

In addition to the Dominican Fair in August, other cultural and sporting events take place throughout the year but tend to be of more special interest. Most events take place from July through to September with autumn the least busy time. Here is a selection of the biggest and most interesting.

Feta Festival

Tell your mates you're off to the Feta festival in Gdansk, and they may wonder about your sudden interest in goat's cheese. The International Festival of Open Air and Street Theatre, to give its full title, has nothing to do with Greek dairy produce and a lot to do with fun and games and a carnival atmosphere in the streets of the Gdansk Main Town. Expect non-stop outdoor over-egged theatre performances, mime artists pushing against invisible brick walls, stilt walkers, dancers and carnival acts, but no cheese. The show kicks off in mid-July and lasts for five days.

Most of the action happens on Długi Targ, Długa Street, Targ Węglowy and Mariacka Street. ⓦ www.feta.pl

Bay of Gdansk Days

This festival of all things maritime takes place every year in early September. It's really a week of regattas, windsurfing, motorboat racing and other water sports, but there's also a beach volleyball competition and various exhibitions on a marine theme accompanied by various side events to keep landlubbers interested. The salty theme continues at various places along the coast including Hel Gdynia and Sopot. ⓦ www.dnizatoki.pl

Topienie Marzanny

Drowning the *Marzanna* (winter witch), a throwback to pagan days, can be witnessed across the Slavic world at the end of March, but could be particularly spectacular by the sea.

PUBLIC HOLIDAYS
New Year's Day 1 January
Easter Sunday and Monday Late March, early April
Labour Day 1 May
Constitution Day 3 May
Assumption 15 August
All Saints' Day 1 November
Independence Day 11 November
Christmas Day 25 December (Christmas Eve is celebrated more than Christmas Day, and is the traditional day for eating Christmas dinner (usually carp). Strangely, Christmas Eve is not a public holiday, whereas Christmas Day is.)

The Dominican Fair

Known as the *Jarmark św. Dominika* in Polish, this is by far Gdansk's biggest annual get-together and a real crowd puller attracting up to 150,000 visitors a day, according to organisers' estimates. It's also the longest-running event by a Swedish mile. It all started in 1260 when Pope Alexander IV gave the Dominican order the power to forgive the sins of those who donated to church funds, the so-called system of indulgences. To celebrate, the monks held a fair, which grew into an important trade event during the city's commercial heyday. Originally held on the Plac Dominikański, it has now spread out to occupy much of the Main Town and is getting bigger and longer every year.

Today the fair is really just an excuse for a three-week-long summer bash in the streets of the Main Town, during which tourists are relieved of their cash. Around 1,000 stalls are crammed into Gdansk's old streets and squares and along the waterfront, selling all sorts of goods including amber, jewellery, local crafts, food, collectables, antiques and large amounts of assorted flotsam and jetsam. There are also round-the-clock performances, rock and pop concerts, firework displays, sports contests and events to suit every age and interest. The fair coincides with the main influx of tourists into the city and a couple of other classical music festivals making Gdansk a hot, heaving sea of people in summer. Needless to say, getting a room in the first three weeks of August requires booking well ahead.

The fair has been organised by the Gdansk International Fair Co since 1996. Check their website for further details.
Ⓦ www.mtgsa.pl

🔺 *Bric-a-brac for sale at the Dominican Fair*

History

THE CITY'S BEGINNINGS

The place where the Wisła River enters the Baltic Sea has always been of strategic importance. The first Slavic settlers arrived here in the 10th century, followed by the Teutonic Knights in the 14th century who colonised the town with Germans. Danzig, as it was then known, thrived on sea trade, and by the mid-15th century was a prosperous member of the Hanseatic League and a citystate with a cosmopolitan population.

During the 16th and late-18th centuries, trade was booming, and Danzig's Eastland Company was even a match for Britain's East India Company. Dutch and Flemish architects built fine town houses, and religious tolerance attracted people fleeing persecution from all over Europe. But, following the partition of Poland in the 1790s, Danzig was seized by Prussia, cutting it off from the source of its export trade.

GDANSK'S MOST FAMOUS SONS

Possibly the most famous name Gdansk has given the world is Daniel Fahrenheit, who was born in the city in 1686. If anyone is unsure about his claim to fame, he invented the Fahrenheit unit of measuring temperature. Günter Grass is also a native of Gdansk and captured life in Danzig during the years of the Free City in his novel *The Tin Drum*. The most celebrated Gdansk resident of our time is Lech Wałęsa, who founded the Solidarity movement in the early 1980s and later became Polish president.

Following World War I, the Treaty of Versailles created the Free City of Danzig at the end of the 'Polish Corridor', a strip of land that cut through Germany, giving Poland access to the sea. This was always a sore point with Hitler, and Danzig's Free City status came to an abrupt end on 1 September 1939 when the German navy fired the first shots of World War II in an attack on the Polish garrison at the Westerplatte.

Danzig was liberated by Soviet forces in March 1945 after a bombardment that left the city a smouldering pile of rubble. The ethnic German population were booted out, Danzig was officially changed to Gdansk, the historical centre was pieced back together, and the shipyards were expanded by the new communist authorities. A decade of disquiet across Poland in the 1970s led to the Lenin Shipyard strike in 1980, which gave birth to Solidarity (Solidarność) led by Lech Wałęsa. Solidarity knocked the first brick out of a shaky communist wall, which collapsed in spectacular fashion, taking all the other Eastern Bloc countries with it.

Despite Poland's economic woes, the city is flourishing and attracting an increasing number of tourists and foreign investors.

🔺 *Solidarity played a key role in the fall of communism*

Lifestyle

Despite living in small prefab flats, having to negotiate the country's crumbling road network, having nothing but reruns of dire US series on TV and watching prices rise and their wages remain stagnant, Poles are an easy-going, amicable, open lot who still show curiosity for and hospitality towards foreigners. Life is relatively tough for all but a small (but growing) middle class, and Poles will quite often hold down a job, study at two universities at once and be teaching something or other to someone or other while bringing up two children, renovating their flats and building a weekend house by a lake somewhere (and not grumble too much). Poles are an optimistic nation, open to new ideas and people. They are also incredibly educated, cultured and well-read, putting most people in the west to shame with their wide knowledge base.

Poles will light up a cigarette absolutely anywhere – on buses, trains, in the four-table breakfast room of a small boutique hotel, while behind the wheel ... perhaps the only place they wouldn't is in church, though you never know. If the Poles put less tar in their lungs and more on their pothole-riddled roads, everyone would be happier. Smokers have nothing to fear in Poland and find at least some relief from their oppressive nanny states. Alcohol, namely vodka, doesn't enjoy the popularity it once did, with the younger generations, especially in the cities, turning to beer.

Of course one of the biggest influences in the life of most Poles is religion in the form of the Catholic Church. Poland seems to have a church on every street corner; Sundays see crowds of people in their best clothes flocking to already packed pews, and nuns and priests and other church dignitaries are a common sight on the country's streets. This might all seem a little disconcerting for more easy-going Anglo-Saxons, but cynical humour about religion will land you in hot water and is not appreciated.

When meeting a Pole, expect him or her to arrive an irritating 15 minutes late. Never give an even number of flowers, as this is reserved for funerals.

⬤ *Gdansk street café*

Culture

Despite its gritty, working-class, ship-building image, Gdansk has a lot to offer on the cultural front. Gdansk as the capital of the Province of Pomerania acts as a cultural hub for a large chunk of Poland, and the city's thousand-year-long colourful history of multiculturalism, religious tolerance and maritime trade combined with a good standard of venues means there's more than enough to keep culture junkies high during a visit any time of year.

Poland has a very highly educated and cultured population. Poles are knowledgeable about their own culture and that of the wider world. They expect a high standard of music, theatre and dance across the country, and the Tri-City is no exception. The arts were well-funded during the communist years, and this has continued to a certain extent to the present day.

Gdansk is possibly at its cultural best during the Dominican Fair (see page 14) when the city comes to life with performances of all kinds. However, the Tri-City also witnesses an organ festival throughout the summer at Oliwa Cathedral, a Shakespeare Festival in August, a Jewish Culture Festival in August, opera, jazz, dance and theatre festivals plus many other smaller events throughout the year. Beach and open-air performances in Sopot and Gdynia are very common, especially in summer (obviously). Check out the listings in *Gdansk In Your Pocket* Ⓦ www.inyourpocket.com or enquire at the tourist information office for more information and dates etc.

◔ *An impromptu musical performance*

The Tri-City has its fair share of museums and galleries, though these don't warrant a visit to the city on their own merit. Remember that many of these places close on Mondays.

However unoriginal the idea may seem, taking a guided tour of the Tri-City or any of its constituent parts is not as sleep-inducing as it may sound. Very often local guides know more interesting little scraps about their city than any guidebook author could ever unearth. Joining a group may be taking it a bit far, but private guides can be hired from PTTK, who allegedly provide guiding services in 15 languages. They run three set tours lasting three, six and eight hours, the last of which includes all the main sights of the Tri-City, ideal for those with just a single day in the area.

PTTK ⓐ ul. Długa 45 ⓣ 058 301 91 51 ⓦ www.pttk-gdansk.pl ⓔ biuro@pttk-gdansk.pl

Citizens of the Tri-City will be quick to tell you of Sopot's reputation as a rock concert venue. Almost every year the town hosts some megastar or other. In 2006 Elton John performed there and other truly big names have also drawn huge summer crowds escaping the heat of Warsaw and other cities.

▶ *A graceful statue reaches for the skies in front of the Main Town Hall*

Shopping

The Tri-City is not exactly a shopper's mecca, but there are a couple of interesting and unusual items, which could add weight to your suitcase on the way home. The 'Gold of the Baltic', namely amber, is sold all over northern Poland. Though it looks like a stone, it is in fact fossilised resin, which oozed out of a tree 40–60 million years ago, capturing bits of leaves and insects as it went. The largest deposits in the world are found on the Baltic coast, though much of it comes from the Russian enclave of Kaliningrad and not Poland at all. Beware, fake amber is so simple to produce from plastic and even sugar. The best methods of telling fake from real are burning, piercing with a red-hot needle and using UV light, not exactly sensible options in a shop. Even licking it or scratching it won't go down well with the shop assistant (especially if he's selling fake stuff). The best advice is not to buy anything that looks too perfect and always choose a shop over a dodgy street stall.

Gdansk's other signature souvenir is *Goldwasser*, a 40 per cent proof root and herbal liqueur. Pretty unremarkable you might think, but this is not called 'Golden Water' for nothing. Tip a bottle upside down and watch hundreds of flakes of real gold leaf flutter through the clear liquid. Production began in the late 16th century when it was thought that gold had magical medicinal properties. Stag night booze connoisseurs call it 'vodka with bits of gold in it', but it is actually a sweet liqueur and a real headache inducer if drunk in large quantities.

◐ *Dusk falls over the Długi Targ (Long Market)*

Gdansk of course has several large soulless malls housing many of the shops you find back home, but don't expect any bargains. The mammoth glass-and-steel Madison Park, and the more attractive Great Mill in the Old Town, are the best located. For meat, fruit and veg, cheap clothes and assorted low-grade tat, try the covered market also in the Old Town, a neo-Gothic structure that has just been renovated at huge expense.

USEFUL SHOPPING PHRASES

What time do the shops open/close?
O której godzinie otwierają/zamykają, sklepy?
O ktoo-rey go-jee-nyair otvyerayom/za-me-ka-yom skhle-pe?

How much is this?
Ile to kosztuje?
Ee-lair toh ko-shtoo-yeh?

Can I try this on?
Czy mogę to przymierzyć?
Che mo-ghair toh pshe-mye-jech?

My size is ...
Mój rozmiar to ...
Mooy roz-myarh toh ...

I'll take this one, thank you
Poproszę o to
Po-pro-shair o toh

This is too large/too small/too expensive.
  Do you have any others
To jest zbyt duże/zbyt małe/zbyt drogie.
  Czy macie coś in-ne-go
Toh yest zbit doo-jeh/zbit ma-weh/zbit dro-ghyeh.
  Che ma-che cosh in-ne-go?

Eating & drinking

Those who believe Polish food to be a bland procession of potatoes and sauerkraut will be pleasantly surprised by what's now on offer in the country. Polish fare is definitely some of the tastiest in central and Eastern Europe and there are some delicious variations on neighbouring cuisines plus influences ranging from Tartar, Armenian and Lithuanian to Cossack, Hungarian and Jewish.

Breakfast is often a quick and light affair of bread, cheese and tea. Most hotels cater to western tastes by offering the full gambit of breakfast foods. Poles then have snacks or a second breakfast around lunchtime and the main meal of the day is eaten around 16.00 or 17.00. This means that restaurants are empty around the time most tourists get the urge to eat lunch. Start the main meal with dripping on bread with pickled gherkin as a starter, followed by *Żurek*, a sour rye soup with a boiled egg or sausage floating in it, or *Barszcz*, a clear version of Russian Borscht. Typical main dishes include *pierogi* (small dumplings filled with meat, potato, sauerkraut or cheese), *gołąbki* (cabbage leaves stuffed with meat and rice), *golonka* (pork knuckle), duck with apples, *naleśniki* (stuffed pancakes),

PRICE RATING

The price ratings given in this book indicate the approximate cost of a three-course meal for one person, excluding drinks.

£ up to 30zł   **££** 30–60zł   **£££** over 60zł

beef roll with buckwheat, *bigos* (a concoction of sauerkraut and meat) and *kotlet schabowy* (battered pork cutlet). Most dishes in restaurants will come with a few token vegetables, mostly red and white cabbage. Poles also love their *grzyby* (mushrooms), which feature heavily on many menus. For dessert, be sure to try Polish cheesecake or apple cake (especially in autumn) often served hot with ice cream. Due to its seaside location Gdansk restaurants have a wider variety of seafood on offer than in many other parts of Poland.

OUTDOOR EATING

In summer, many restaurants and cafés provide outdoor seating under huge parasols, more often than not emblazoned with the logo of a popular Polish beer. On most Polish main squares these

🔺 *The infamous Żubrówka (Bison grass vodka) and local beers*

parasol cities merge into one another, forming an impenetrable barrier between the square and the surrounding houses.

Of course, with so many beaches around the Gulf of Gdansk, picnicking by the Baltic in fine weather is a cheap and fun option. Stock up on picnic food from any supermarket or fruit and veg stall.

DRINKING CULTURE

The Poles down gallons of *herbata* (tea) per person every year, and it is by far the most popular hot drink. Black tea dominates, but herbal and fruit teas are growing in popularity. *Kawa* (coffee) is as good as it gets in this part of the world, and the locals love a comforting mug of thick, hot cocoa as well. Fruit juices and cola are popular soft drinks. You may have heard that the Poles are vodka addicts, knocking back shots before breakfast and similar tales. This is now a bit of a stereotype and while vodka consumption is high among the over 40s, vodka fatigue is making the younger generations turn to *piwo* (beer). However, don't leave Poland without trying a shot of *Żubrówka* (Bison grass vodka) with apple juice (known as a *szarlotka*) and unbelievably inexpensive bottles of vodka and Goldwasser make great souvenirs. Poland's beer market, though no match for the Czechs' to the south, is booming, and the most common brands are *Żywiec*, *Tyskie*, *Okocim*, *Lech*, *Tatra* and *Żubr*. Gdansk has its own quite palatable Heweliusz brand. Your half-litre of fermented hop juice sometimes comes with complimentary bread, dripping and salt. Polish wine is at best drinkable and is hardly available anyway, as it is produced in just a tiny region in the west of the country.

TIPPING

Poland has no tipping culture, but rounding the bill up to the nearest 5 or 10 złoty is a simple way of showing you were happy with the food and service. Menus are only occasionally in English.

USEFUL DINING PHRASES

I'd like a table for people
Poprozę o stolik dla ... osób
Po-pro-shair o sto-leek dla ... o-soob

May I have the bill please?
Poproszę o rachunek?
Po-pro-shair o ra-hoo-neck

Waiter/waitress!
Kelner/Kelnerka!
Kelner/Kelnerka!

Could I have it well-cooked/medium/rare, please
Poproszę o dobrze/średnio/lekko wysmażone?
Po-pro-shair o do-bjeh/shre-dnyo/lek-ko ve-sma-jo-ne?

I am a vegetarian. Does this contain meat?
Jetsem wegetarianinem/wegetarianką (fem.).
    Czy w tym daniu jest mieęso?
Yestem vegetarianinem/vegetariankahng (fem.).
    Tche fteem dah-nyoo yest myensoh?

Where is the toilet (restroom), please?
Przepraszam, gdzie jest toaleta?
Pshe-pra-sham ghjair yest toe-a-lair-tah?

Entertainment & nightlife

NIGHTLIFE TRI-CITY STYLE

One of the most exciting aspects of the Tri-City is its wild nightlife scene. Sopot in particular, with its disproportionate number of clubs and bars lining the beach (see page 112) and the main street, is a magnet for young Poles and foreigners looking for a night out that just wouldn't be experienced anywhere else in Poland. In the summer months it seems as though half of Warsaw has escaped from the dreary, heat-exhausted capital to find fun and frolics in the refreshing Baltic breeze. Sopot must be one of central and Eastern Europe's greatest party towns, if not the greatest, with the fun bursting out onto the beach and merging into one vodka-fuelled Baltic bash. Gdansk also gets in on the act with a few super cool venues and a couple of easy-going dance floors. Superbly conceived clubs, a great party atmosphere, DJs from east and west and the chance to swim naked in the Baltic – and all for a fraction of what you would have to shell out back home to have this good a time.

OTHER ENTERTAINMENT

Naturally the Tri-City has less raucous forms of entertainment. Jazz is relatively big throughout the conurbation, and in summer there are jazz festivals in both Sopot and Gdansk, as well as regular live sessions at Gdansk's Cotton Club. The Baltic Philharmonic Hall holds regular chamber concerts and the State Baltic Opera near the Politechnika Station of the SKM has a wide-ranging repertoire. If you do go to the opera, be aware that

The party never stops in Sopot

the subtitles will be in Polish. Some opera-goers are quite taken aback by this quite obvious aspect of opera abroad, though it's not so bad if you already know the plot. For more information on opera listings, visit these websites:

Baltic Philharmonic Hall ⓦ www.filharmonia.gda.pl
State Baltic Opera ⓦ www.operabaltycka.pl

The Forest Opera in Sopot (see page 111) is home to a variety of non-operatic performances, including the annual Sopot International Song Contest. Built in 1909, and set outdoors in beautiful woodlands, it's an amazing amphitheatre that can seat around 4,000 people – the acoustics are fantastic. Performances range from plays (operatic and theatrical) to big-name bands and artists.

Cinema is also an option for non-Poles as hardly any films are dubbed into Polish for the silver screen (alas, not true for TV).
Multikino ⓐ Al. Zwycięstwa 14 ⓣ 058 340 30 99
ⓦ www.multikino.pl
Kino Polonia (Sopot) ⓐ ul. Bohaterów Monte Cassino 55/57
ⓣ 058 551 05 34

Theatre is not really an option for visitors from abroad unless they happen to understand Polish. There can be nothing less entertaining than watching a play in a foreign language that you don't understand. You find yourself looking at the light fittings and way out signs very early on in the performance.

If simply soaking up the city's atmosphere in bars and terraces is more your style, you won't be disappointed. The choice of beer on offer is numerous, and you are unlikely to have strayed too far from a carb-fuelled menu from which to choose your soak-up food of preference.

⬤ *Unusual bar in Głowne Miasto (Main Town)*

Sport & relaxation

WATER SPORTS

The sea plays a major role in sport and leisure activities in the Tri-City, with activities as diverse as kayaking, sailing, cod fishing, parasailing, waterskiing, wakeboarding, sea banana riding, sailing, wreck-diving and just good old-fashioned swimming and paddling also possible. To arrange any of the above, contact **Joytrip** Ⓦ www.joytrip.pl, a one-stop Gdansk-based leisure company, or **Extrem** on Sopot beach ❶ 060 312 08 88, who specialise in boat hire and other water sports.

OTHER ACTIVITIES

Away from the cold Baltic briny, there's horseracing at Sopot racecourse and horse riding and cycle trips into the hinterland. Football is not that big in the Tri-City with Lechia Gdansk, winners of the Polish cup in 1983, now plying their trade in the second division, and Arka Gdynia struggling in the first. Matches are normally played on Saturday evenings, and tickets are incredibly cheap (around 30zł). For golfers, the Postołowo golf course has a very high standard of facilities, though is difficult to reach without a car as it is situated 26 km (16 miles) south of Gdansk in the village of Postołowo: ❶ 058 683 71 00 Ⓦ www.golf.com.pl

Perhaps the best way to relax and unwind in the Tri-City is just to stroll along the region's beaches, enjoy a barbecue by the shore or sunbathe (when the Baltic wind is having a day off). Why not hire a bike, pack a picnic and head off with friends to the coast for a day of picnicking, swimming and building sandcastles. If you get sick of the sand in your sandwiches, you can always head back to town to visit the zoo and park in the suburb of Oliwa, take a cruise on a pirate ship from Sopot pier, have a splash around at the **Aquapark in Sopot** ⓦ www.aquaparksopot.pl or enjoy an evening of bowling and pool at the **Centrum U7 Gdansk** ⓦ www.u7.pl

● *The Baltic coast offers perfect conditions for windsurfing*

Accommodation

Gdansk now has a fairly good range of hotels and other accommodation, and every year sees a couple of new hotels hoist the omnipresent flags of welcome nationalities above their doors. The range covers all pockets and requirements, from 5-star lunacy to camping at the beach, and from bog-standard soulless to baroque boutique. The city does suffer from a slight lack of hostel accommodation in the summer months, but this is made up for by the availability of student halls. Most hotels are in the city centre, meaning the Main and Old Towns. Prices are often quoted in euros, but you will be expected to pay in złoty. Booking ahead in the summer months, particularly during the Dominican Fair, is just common sense.

CAMPING

Stogi Camping Site £ The best of Gdansk's camping grounds with one of the city's best beaches nearby. It's around 5 km (3 miles) from the city centre at the end of tramline No. 8.
ⓐ ul. Wydmy 9 ☏ 058 307 39 15 ☎ 058 304 22 59 ⌚ May–Sept
Ⓝ Tram: No. 8.

> **PRICE RATING**
> All prices are for a single night in a double or twin room.
> **£** up to 200zł **££** 200–500zł **£££** over 500zł

HOSTELS

Dizzy Daisy £ The Gdansk branch of the Dizzy Daisy chain is well-located in the Old Town, a few hundred metres from the railway station. There are 15 sparklingly clean doubles, 4 dorms and several other rooms of varying sizes. No curfew and 24-hour reception. ⓐ Gnilna 3 ⓣ 058 301 39 19 ⓦ www.hostel.pl ⓔ gdansk@hostel.pl

Hostel Przy Targu Rybnym £ Guests at the 'Fish Market Hostel' rave about the freebies such as internet access, use of bikes and even free kayak hire. It must have one of the liveliest common rooms on Poland's backpacking circuit and one of the friendliest and most hands-on owners. You can choose to sleep in the dorm, which has beds packed like sardines (well, this is the fish market), and five other more spacious rooms. The dorm is not a place for those who like any level of privacy. All in all a great place with a real backpacker flavour, situated in a prime location just off the waterfront. ⓐ ul. Grodzka 21 ⓣ 058 301 56 27 ⓦ www.gdanskhostel.com ⓔ gdanskhostel@hotmail.com

APARTMENTS

Gdansk Apartments ££ The GA guys have some superb properties to rent throughout the Main Town. They sleep from 1–8 people, and all are recently renovated. Single-night stays are not a problem, though this sort of accommodation lends itself to longer-term sojourns. There's a whopping 45 per cent discount if you stay for one month. ⓣ 050 305 71 42 ⓦ www.warsawshotel.com/gdansk-hotels.htm ⓔ gdanskota@hotmail.com

○ Hotel Podewils is in the heart of the historic waterfront area

Willa Isabel ££ The Isabel is something special and well worth considering if you don't mind staying a short distance outside the city centre. Standing on raised ground, this huge villa housing seven apartments has first-rate views of the historical centre. Each apartment has a different colour theme and is littered with carefully selected antiques. Guests can also sip from the wine cellar and blacken Polish sausages on the BBQ. ⓐ Ul. Na Zboczu 67A ⓣ 058 300 05 70 ⓦ www.willa-isabel.pl ⓔ biuro@willa-isabel.pl ⓝ Bus: 118, 155, 255, 295, 208

HOTELS

Dom Muzyka ££ Housed in a former music academy, the newly created House of Music is a cheap and cheerful place, a short walk from the main action. Some of the spick and span rooms are on the small side and lack character, but the breakfast is generous and the English-speaking staff obliging enough. ⓐ ul. Łąkowa 1/2 ⓣ 058 326 06 00 ⓦ www.dom-muzyka.pl ⓔ biuro@dom-muzyka.pl

Kamienica Gotyk ££ Certainly one of the best-located and inexpensive places to stay in Gdansk. Occupying the oldest house in town, the front door leads directly onto picturesque Mariacka Street, a position that would be the envy of many a top-class establishment. Book early as there are just five rooms. ⓐ ul. Mariacka 1 ⓣ 058 301 85 67 ⓦ www.gotykhouse.eu ⓔ reservation@gotykhouse.eu

Hotel Królewski ££ This is an interesting hotel housed in a rebuilt granary on Ołowianka Island. Behind the tiny windows

are 30 smart rooms of a higher standard than the room rate suggests. There are pretty views of Gdansk's old centre from the upper floors and an excellent restaurant on the premises.
ⓐ ul. Ołowianka 1 ⓣ 058 326 11 11 ⓦ www.hotelkrolewski.pl
ⓔ info@hotelkrolewski.pl

Hotel Wolne Miasto ££ The 'Free City' provides a higher standard of accommodation than the price tag would suggest and is one of the best deals in Gdansk. The reception with its huge, dark-wood desk and discreetly imbedded PC screens hints at what's to come in the rooms. Beautifully presented doubles and singles with top-notch furnishings and fittings make you feel you're paying a lot more than you are. ⓐ ul. Świętego Ducha 2
ⓣ 058 322 24 41 ⓦ www.hotelwm.pl ⓔ rezerwacja@hotelwm.pl

Podewils £££ The 5-star Podewils is a seriously stylish hotel on the banks of the Motława River, that manages to combine elegance and charm with modernity and practicality. Plush rooms, all mod cons, dutiful staff and an opulent fragrance in the air make this the place to stay if you've money and style to burn. ⓐ ul. Szafarnia 2 ⓣ 058 300 95 60
ⓦ www.podewils-hotel.pl ⓔ gdansk@podewils-hotel.pl

THE BEST OF GDANSK

Whether you're spending just one night in this the city or are planning a more leisurely break here, there are several places that should not be missed.

TOP 10 ATTRACTIONS

- **Sopot's nightlife scene** One of the best nightlife spots in central and Eastern Europe with club after club lighting up the Baltic. Not to be missed (see page 115).

- **Wandering Gdansk's historical centre** It's all rebuilt, but you'd never guess (see page 60).

- **Sopot pier – the longest wooden pier in the world** In Sopot everyone knows that size *does* matter (see page 110).

- **The Hel Peninsula** Take the road to Hel (so this is what Chris Rea was singing about!) (see page 107).

- **A tasty traditional meal in a restaurant** Whether it's local fish or a dish from the hinterland, Polish food is truly the best in the region (see page 27).

- **Atmospheric Mariacka Street** Experience the atmosphere of pre-war Gdansk (see page 60).

- **Goldwasser** The taste of gold. Isn't swallowing flakes of gold leaf bad for you? Possibly not as bad as the 40 per cent liqueur it's floating in (see page 24).

- **The Solidarity Museum** Yes, an electrician with a moustache really did change Europe forever (see page 82).

- **Catching an organ concert in Oliwa Cathedral** Free organ concerts in the Gothic cathedral in Gdansk's leafy Oliwa district (see page 94).

- **The August Dominican Fair** Gdansk goes barmy in the balmy summer air with streets packed with stalls, theatre performers and a sea of tourists (see page 14).

▼ *The pretty waterfront lies at the heart of historic Gdansk*

HALF-DAY: GDANSK IN A HURRY

Half a day really limits you to the sights of Gdansk's Main and Old Towns. You could definitely squeeze in the city's prettiest thoroughfares – Długa Street and Długi Targ as well as the waterfront and Mariacka Street, where you could stop for a bite to eat in one of the outdoor cafés. At a push you could then take a taxi to Oliwa to see the cathedral and parks.

1 DAY: TIME TO SEE A LITTLE MORE

One day gives you much more scope to explore. Spend the morning as above, then in the afternoon catch the commuter train from the main railway station to Sopot for a leisurely stroll down the main street lined with shops and outdoor cafés to the pier. After a 500 m (1,640 ft) walk out to sea along its wooden length, head back, then take a left or right to get sand in your shoes on the beach. End the day at a restaurant in either Sopot or Gdansk, sampling some tasty Polish victuals and a few shots of Goldwasser or Żubrówka before heading to a club to round off the night in the company of gyrating young Poles.

2–3 DAYS: SHORT CITY BREAK

This length of time is a full-blown city break and means you can probably squeeze in the above plus trips to Malbork Castle and up to the thin streak of sandbank called the Hel Peninsula by train or what the locals call a water tram (a boat in other words). You can also fit in a trip to see Gdansk's famous lighthouse, the first building to be damaged in World War II, and possibly the Westerplatte.

LONGER: ENJOYING GDANSK TO THE FULL

A week in the Tri-City would enable the Baltic enthusiast to explore Gdansk, Sopot, Malbork and the Hel Peninsula, as well as discover some of the less visited corners of the Gulf of Gdansk, such as the port city of Gdynia and the seaside villages of Puck, Jastrzębia Góra and Jastarnia. Longer excursions to the Kashubia Region to the south and the dunes of the Słowiński National Park to the west are also feasible.

🔺 *The narrow-fronted houses of Długi Targ (Long Market)*

Something for nothing

They didn't call this the Free City for nothing, and much of what Gdansk has to offer won't cost you a grosz, just a bit of legwork. This is very much a city for strolling around with much of the centre semi-pedestrianised. Immersing yourself in the maze of streets that make up the Main Town doesn't cost a thing, and no tourist authority on earth has yet come up with a method for charging visitors to look at historical monuments from the outside.

The best things in life usually don't involve a credit card, and this is particularly true in Sopot. Bury each other in the white sand, turn purple in the Baltic's icy briny and have sand blown between your teeth on Sopot's fine stretch of seashore. Even the ticket sellers abandon their booths on the pier when skies are leaden, and anyone can wander on and off the wooden expanse at will.

Poland's churches are always open (and full of people) and, with some infamous exceptions, never charge admission. Gdansk is packed with red-brick Gothic churches that can be explored for zilch. The pick of the bunch is Oliwa Cathedral where you can even enjoy a free concert of organ music (though occasionally they may try to extract 5 złoty out of you) before discovering the surrounding landscaped parkland.

Polish museums also regularly extend the hand of charity to the financially challenged. Almost every museum in the country has one day in the week when admission charges are dropped, and Gdansk is no exception. The bulk of events held on the city's streets, including street theatre and concerts, are also a great way of enjoying Gdansk without a złoty piece to your name.

The shipyards and Monument to Fallen Shipyard Workers don't cost a sausage, and approaching the Roads to Freedom exhibition there is an open-air exhibition of photographs from the strikes and various other artefacts including a genuine piece of the Berlin Wall (no chipping bits off!).

⬤ *It's not always Baltic on Sopot beach*

When it rains

When it rains (and it often does) buy an umbrella and continue with what you had planned regardless, or else take shelter in one of the city's museums and galleries. If these happen to be closed the day the heavens open, churches provide literally minutes of entertainment until the sun reappears, though you may get a soaking walking between them. You never know, you may be lucky enough to catch a service in Polish (though you may not find a free pew in this country).

The most obvious choice for a long-haul drizzly museum day is the wonderful Gdansk branch of the National Museum located in the cheerless so-called Old Suburb (Stare Przedmieście) just to the south of the Main Town. The building is part of a former Franciscan Monastery and inside you'll find heaps of paintings, gold and silverware and local crafts plus a collection of bulky Danzig-style cupboards, which have cleverly concealed keyholes as they were used primarily to store precious chunks of amber. Another museum worth its salt is the Amber Museum. Housed in the Foregate to Długa Street it holds lumps of 'Gdansk Gold' whittled, chipped, carved and polished into a myriad of shapes and sizes.

Sopot is not the best place to be caught on a rainy day. The best place to head for in this unhappy state of affairs is the Krzywy Dom (or Centrum Rezydent as nobody calls it) packed chock-a-block with trendy cafés, pubs and snack bars. You could also try the Kawiarnia u Hrabiego where there is a small gallery.

Malbork Castle is the place to be in a downpour, as you'll be protected from the elements by metre-thick Gothic red-brick walls. The three-hour tours in Polish will keep you distracted (or drive you to distraction), and if the rain is still falling when you emerge, retreat to the Piwniczka Restaurant within the castle walls to sink a few Polish wet ones.

⬥ *Retreat to Malbork Castle if it rains*

On arrival

Gdansk, and indeed the whole of Poland, is in a time zone 1 hour ahead of Greenwich Mean Time, and the clocks go forward one hour for daylight saving in March, and back again in October. When it's midday in summer in Gdansk, the time elsewhere is as follows:

Australia Eastern Standard Time 20.00, Central Standard Time 19.30, Western Standard Time 18.00

New Zealand 22.00

South Africa 12.00

UK and Republic of Ireland 11.00

USA and Canada Newfoundland Time 07.30, Atlantic Canada Time 07.00, Eastern Time 06.00, Central Time 05.00, Mountain Time 04.00, Pacific Time 01.00, Alaska 02.00.

Długie Pobrzeże

◗ *Detail of a waterfront house*

ARRIVING

By air

Gdansk's small Lech Wałęsa Airport is located 14 km (9 miles) west of the city Ⓦ www.airport.gdansk.pl. Journey times to the city centre by taxi are anyone's guess and depend heavily on the time of day. At present if you land between 15.00 and 18.00 you'll be stuck in traffic for literally hours. Bus B and night bus N3 run between the airport and Gdansk Main bus station. Tickets are valid for a certain number of minutes so to make absolutely sure your ticket doesn't run out halfway to the centre, buy a 4.20zł ticket from the driver.

By rail

All trains terminate at Gdansk Glówny station just to the west of the Old Town. To reach the Old Town, cross the main Podwale Grodzkie Road and head down Karmelicka and Heweliusza Streets until you hit Rajska. To reach the Main Town from there, turn right and follow Rajska (which changes names several times) until you get to the Golden Gate and the top of Długa Street.

By bus

The bus station is situated behind the railway station and linked to it by an underground passageway.

FINDING YOUR FEET

The Tri-City is as safe as anywhere in Poland, which generally has low levels of crime. Petty theft should be your main concern, so keep an eye on your possessions at stations, on the train to

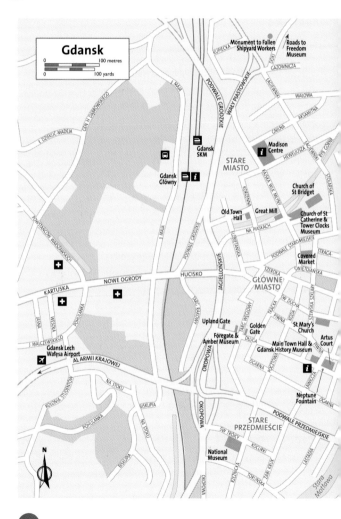

Gdansk

0 — 100 metres
0 — 100 yards

Monument to Fallen Shipyard Workers
Roads to Freedom Museum

KUPIECKA
GAZOWNICZA
WATOWA
LACHOWA
AKSAMITNA
I MAŁA
CNILNA
PODWALE GRODZKIE
WAŁY PIASTOWSKIE
JEWELUSZA ACHMINNA
RYE GÓRNE

Gdansk SKM
Madison Centre
STARE MIASTO

Gdansk Główny
Church of St Bridget

KORZENNA
RAJSKA WIEE MURY
Old Town Hall
Great Mill
Church of St Catherine & Tower Clocks Museum

ELBIANSKA
NA PIASKACH

PODWALE CRODZKIE
PODWALE STAROMIEJSKIE
STRACA
Covered Market
SZEROKA
ŚWIETOJANSKA

NOWE OGRODY
HUCISKO
JAGIELLOŃSKIE
GŁÓWNE MIASTO

KARTUSKA
POKULANKA
TARG RAKOWY
KALCA
SW. DUCHA
JOSIA
SZAŃSKA SZKLAR

JANA
WESOLA
PIWNA

Upland Gate
Golden Gate
St Mary's Church

Foregate & Amber Museum
DELUCA
Main Town Hall & Gdansk History Museum
Artus Court

J. MALCZEWSKIEGO
Gdansk Lech Wałesa Airport
AL ARMII KRAJOWEJ
OCARNA
PIWNA

KOLONIA STUDENTÓW
NA STOKU
BISKUPIA
Neptune Fountain
OCARNA

OKOPOWA
STARE PRZEDMIEŚCIE
PODWALE PRZEDMIEJSKIE

POPULANKA
NA STOKU
SW. TRÓJCY
KOCURKI

National Museum
RZELNICZA
TORUNSKA
JABI WIUK
LASTADIA

Stara Motlawa

N

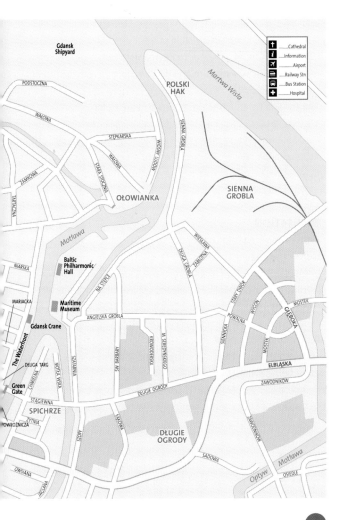

Sopot and in crowds. Theft from cars is all too common, so never leave your belongings in a visible place.

Perhaps more of a danger to newcomers to the Tri-City is the area's roads. Cross with care and don't expect drivers to stop on zebra crossings.

In today's Poland, beggars, alas, form an all too common welcoming party for tourists (and locals). Poles are a charitable bunch and often drop a few grosz into their cut-off McDonalds paper cup. To give or not to give? It's up to you, but you may be indirectly funding a drug habit or a close relative's Mercedes.

ORIENTATION

Gdansk is divided into the *Główne Miasto* (Main Town) with most of the historical places of interest, the main shopping streets, cafés, bars and restaurants, and the *Stare Miasto* (Old Town) to the north of that squeezed between the Main town and Gdansk's famous shipyard. Beyond that are the suburbs of Oliwa, Zaspa and Wrzeszcz until you reach the holiday resort and nightlife hotspot of Sopot. The Motława River twists its way to the sea through the city centre where it forms several islands before being swallowed by the Baltic.

Should you get lost, a good point to head for is the spire of the Church of St Mary, the highest structure in the Main Town, visible from almost anywhere.

CAR HIRE

This is a city of narrow streets, many of which are pedestrianised in the city centre, with a handy and cheap system of public transport. Hiring a car is probably unnecessary, unless you want the convenience of having your own set of wheels for a jaunt down to Malbork Castle 50 km (31 miles) to the southeast. Gdansk's road network is a work in progress and will be for the foreseeable future, making even the shortest journey a real test of patience. Generally, driving in Poland is definitely not for the faint-hearted as Polish drivers have something of a death wish, and the roads are the worst in the region (even Ukraine has better).

These are the best car rental companies to try:

Car hire companies
Avis ⓐ ul. Słowackiego 200 (Lech Wałęsa Airport)
ⓣ 058 348 12 89 ⓦ www.avis.pl ⓔ gdansk_lotnisko@avis.pl

IF YOU GET LOST, TRY ...

Excuse me, do you speak English?
Przepraszam, czy mówi Pan/Pani po angielsku?
Pshe-pra-sham che moo-vee Pan/Pa-nee poe an-gyels-koo?

**Excuse me, is this the right way to the old town/
the city centre/the tourist office/the train station/
the bus station?**
Przepraszam, czy dojdę tędy do starego miasta/
centrum miasta/biura turystycznego/dworzec kolejowy/
dworca autobusowego?
*Pshe-pa-sham che doy-dair ten-di doe sta-re-go mya-stah/
sten-troom mya-stah/byoo-rah too-ri-sti-chne-go/
dvo-zhets ko-le-yo-vi/dvortsah awto-boo-so-vego?*

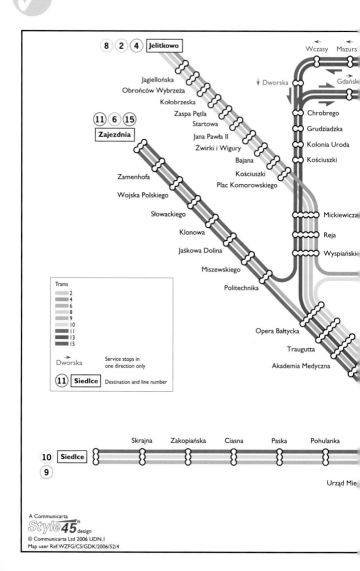

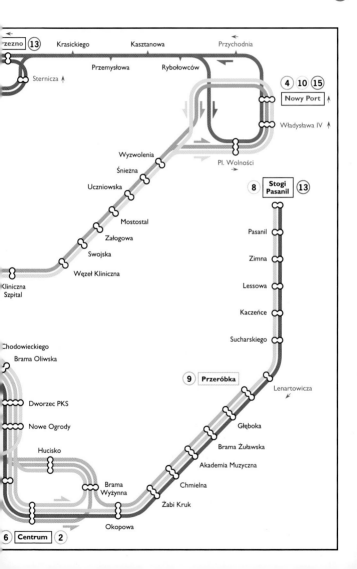

Hertz @ ul. Słowackiego 200 (Lech Wałęsa Airport)
t 058 301 40 45 **w** www.hertz.com.pl **e** gdansk@hertz.com.pl
JOKA Car Rental @ ul. Chmielna 26 **t** 058 320 56 45
w www.joka.com.pl **e** joka@joka.com.pl
National @ Car ul. Słowackiego 200 (Lech Wałęsa Airport)
t 058 660 61 97 **w** www.nationalcar.com.pl
e gdansk@nationalcar.com.pl

GETTING AROUND

The Tri-City conurbation has a very efficient public transport
system with buses, trams and the SKM commuter train
whisking you anywhere you wish to go cheaply and safely. The
last of this trio links up Gdansk, Sopot and the town of Gdynia,
and runs approximately every ten minutes from Gdansk Main
Railway Station. It's the best way to get from the city centre to
Sopot's white sandy beaches and booming nightlife scene.
Handy night services enable you to get back to your hotel after
a night on the tiles. Tickets costing from 2.20zł can be bought in
kiosks and from machines and must be stamped in the yellow
machines at the entrance to stations, otherwise you will be
fined. Saying you're a foreigner, and that you have bought a
ticket, will cut no ice whatsoever. Gdansk's public transport
system is operated by ZKM (Zarząd Transportu Miejskiego)
w www.zkm.pl. Tickets are valid for a certain number of minutes
and must also be stamped on boarding: 10 min = 1.40zł, 30 min
= 2.80zł, 60 min = 4.20zł. A 24-hour ticket costs a mere 9.10zł,
great value.

○ *Colourful frontage, Długi Targ*

Główne Miasto (Main Town)

Gdansk's showpiece district, the Main Town, is by far the most interesting part of the city and the main draw for visitors. Though bombarded to rubble at the end of World War II, it has been painstakingly restored to its 17th- and 18th-century appearance over the six decades since. The restorers were selective in what they rebuilt, and later Prussian additions did not make a re-appearance. This means that, rather curiously, hardly anything you see while strolling around the Main Town is original, though you would never know it. Alas, this is a story repeated across Poland, a country that saw more devastation than possibly any other in Europe during World War II.

SIGHTS & ATTRACTIONS

Mariacka Street
Often dubbed the prettiest street in Poland, Mariacka Street was carefully rebuilt after World War II with every fragment of the rubble incorporated into the new buildings. Its raised patios, wrought-iron railings and odd scraps of carved stone serving as benches give it a wonderful ambience and it is a particularly atmospheric place when under a blanket of snow or the tourists have gone home. It's now lined with amber and handicrafts shops and some great little eateries.

The Royal Way walking tour
The simplest and most economical way to take in the sights of the Main Town is to follow the Royal Way to the waterfront. The

route was used by the kings of Poland on their annual visits to the city to collect taxes and starts at a collection of town gates. The first of these is called the **Upland Gate**, originally built in the 16th century as part of a ring of fortifications. The Upland Gate made the next bulky structure, the **Foregate**, possibly dating from the 13th century, rather redundant. The Foregate housed a prison until 1945 and is still undergoing restoration. The **Golden Gate** stands immediately behind that, and if you think its walls and sculpture look a bit too new and shiny, this is because it was only rebuilt in 1997. Look out for the allegorical statues of Peace, Freedom, Wealth, Fame, Wisdom, Piety, Justice and Concord lining the balustrade on the top.

Having negotiated the gates, you find yourself on **Długa Street**, one of the grandest thoroughfares in the land, reflecting just how wealthy the city once was. Proud, slender six-storey townhouses line the wide, pedestrianised street and end at street level with either a shop or a café with tables, chairs and sunshades spilling out onto the cobbles. It's hard to imagine that in 1945 this was a pile of smoking debris.

The entire way along Długa Street (which despite being called 'Long Street' is only about 300 m (984 ft) in length) you will have the tall, slender spire of the **Main Town Hall** in your sights. The original structure dates from the 14th century but was added to over the next three centuries. In 1945 only some of the outer walls remained, and protests from townspeople persuaded the authorities to rebuild. The spire, the highest in Gdansk at 81 m (266 ft), is topped by a life-size statue of Polish king Zigmunt II August. The building is now home to the Gdansk History Museum (see page 68).

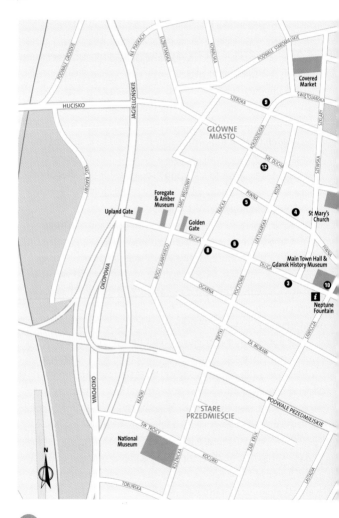

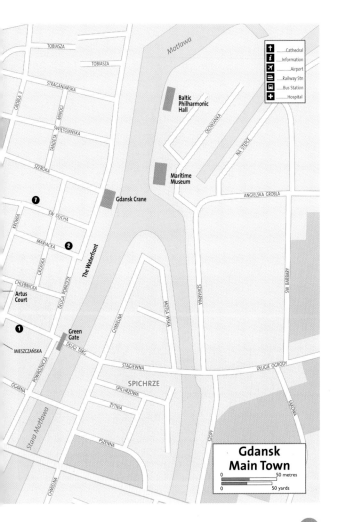

TOBIASZA

TOBIASZA

Motława

STRAGANIARSKA

GROBLA II

MINOGI

SWIĘTOJAŃSKA

TANDETA

SZEROKA

KRWIA

SW. DUCHA

MARIACKA

GRZĄSKA

PIWNA

CHLEBNICKA

Artus Court

MIESZCZAŃSKA

PONROŻNICZA

OGARNA

Stara Motława

The Waterfront

Gdansk Crane

Baltic Philharmonic Hall

Maritime Museum

OKOPOWA

OKOPOWA

NA STĘPCE

ANGIELSKA GROBLA

SZAFARNIA

SW. BARBARY

DŁUGIE PORIEŻE

Green Gate

DŁUGI TARG

STĄGIEWNA

DŁUGIE OGRODY

SPICHRZE

SPICHRZOWA

ŻYTNIA

ŁĄCHA

ŁĄSOŚ

PSZENNA

CHMIELNA

MOTŁAWSKA

CHMIELNA

Gdansk Main Town

0 — 50 metres
0 — 50 yards

Cathedral
Information
Airport
Railway Stn
Bus Station
Hospital

❶ ❷ ❼

◆ The Main Town Hall was rebuilt after World War II

At the foot of the Main Town Hall Długa Street suddenly widens out in to the **Długi Targ** (Long Market), again not very long, probably just longer than all the other markets in the city. Once again, sunshades emblazoned with every Polish beer brand logo going dominate, above which tower more, even thinner, Hanseatic merchants' townhouses painted in a rainbow of colours and with elaborate gables. Tourists and locals mill around on the cobbles and stop for a moment to admire the famous **Neptune Fountain**, created by a Flemish artist, Peter Husen, in the early 17th century.

Immediately behind Neptune, the **Artus Court** commands attention with its white façade, three bold Gothic arches and gilt statues. It was named after King Arthur of the round table as it was founded as a meeting place for merchants and other VIPs in the late 15th century. Blasted to dust in 1945, Gdansk's most desirable address was meticulously restored to its former glory and is now open for the public to view its grand main hall and adjoining chambers, which contain some fine examples of Danzig furniture. The upper floors house an exhibition on the history of the building.

NEPTUNE FOUNTAIN

The black, bearded figure of Neptune, modesty only just covered by some mythical creature's tail, wields a trident, out of the tips of which, as legend would have it, flowed the original Goldwasser (see page 24). Neptune escaped damage during World War II by being hidden away along with many of the city's other treasures.

The Royal Way ends at the **Green Gate** (that isn't green at all), which fills the eastern end of the Long Market. It was constructed in the mid-16th century as a royal residence, but the kings shunned the building and preferred to reside elsewhere on the Long Market. In fact the only head of state to ever use it was Lech Wałęsa, who had an office there. Pass through any of the four arches to reach Gdansk's waterfront.

St Mary's Church

The arresting façades of the Church of St Mary contain what is reckoned to be the largest Gothic brick church in the world, able to hold up to 25,000 people. It has a rather austere interior, interrupted only by various chapels, the altar and an astronomical clock, which was the world's tallest clock when it was completed in 1470. For a small fee you can climb to the top of the tower if you're in good enough shape to negotiate the 402 steps. The views from the top, of Gdansk and the surrounding plains, are worth the ascent.

The Waterfront

The waterfront is no longer busy with barges loading and unloading their cargos of grain and wood, but with crowds of strolling tourists enjoying the outdoor cafés, stalls and shops overlooking the River Motława. Look across the river and you will see the Spichlerze Island, which once held up to 300 granaries. The majority of these were destroyed in 1945 and the bomb damage (some of the most extensive to have survived the intervening 60 years anywhere in Europe) can still be seen. Some have been rebuilt and now house hotels and museums.

● *Neptune stands guard over the streets*

The main attraction on the waterfront is the **Gdansk Crane**, a looming wooden structure overhanging the pavement and dockside. Built in the 15th century, its mechanism involved people walking around huge 'mouse wheels' to lift and lower cargoes onto waiting ships. Though it was the largest crane in medieval Europe, it may leave you wondering what all the fuss is about.

The waterfront's real name is *Długie Pobrzeże* (Long Waterfront) and extends right up to the Fish Market (though it changes its name to Fish Waterfront half way along). Every street that reaches the waterfront from the Main Town ends in a defensive gate. It is through one of these gates (St Mary's) that you enter picturesque Mariacka Street.

CULTURE

Amber Museum
Housed in the Foregate, the newly opened Amber Museum provides inspiration to go out and buy some of the waxy yellow 'stones' (though you won't find many pieces like these incredible exhibits on sale in the streets). Caskets, small statues, candlesticks, bottles, amber in its natural form, jewellery and even a display of fake amber fill the floors of the Prison Tower in the Foregate and are well worth half an hour of perusal.
ⓐ Targ Węglowy ⓦ www.mhmg.gda.pl ⓛ 10.00–18.00 Tues–Sat, 11.00–18.00 Sun, 10.00–15.00 Mon

Gdansk History Museum
The first section of the museum consists of several period

rooms, the most outstanding of which is the Red Room with its magnificent decoration and painted ceiling. The room is an original as it was taken to pieces and hidden during World War II. The second floor houses exhibits on the history of the city, the most interesting being the before and after images of the city in 1945 and today and a Calendar of Destruction tracing the course of Allied bombing raids on the city.

ⓐ ul. Długa 47 🕐 10.00–18.00 Tues–Sat, 11.00–18.00 Sun, 10.00–15.00 Mon

Maritime Museum

The Maritime Museum has various exhibits on both sides of the Motława River including the Gdansk Crane, an exhibition of boats from around the world, a section on Poland's seafaring history and the *Sołdek*, the first ship to be built in Gdansk following World War II. One ticket covers all the various sections, and in summer there's a special museum ferry to transport you to and from the other riverbank.

ⓐ ul. Ołowianka 9–13 ⓦ www.cmm.pl 🕐 10.00–18.00 Tues–Sun, June–Sept; 10.00–15.00/16.00 Tues–Sun, Oct–May

RETAIL THERAPY

Amber and Goldwasser are the sparkling Gdansk duo that many visitors cart home with them. The best places to buy amber are the small shops and stalls in Mariacka Street, Długa Street and Długi Targ. Beware of fakes. The Galeria Venus outlets in Mariacka and on the waterfront specialise in more upmarket products.

◉ *All aboard* Sołdek, *now part of the Maritime Museum*

For traditional Polish arts and crafts the only place to head for is Cepelia on Długa Street. This is not just a country-wide chain of stores that has been going strong for more than 50 years, but an organisation that supports research in art, handicrafts and ethnography, runs galleries, promotes traditional Polish culture abroad and has an array of activities too numerous to mention here. It's a kitsch-free zone, the real folksy deal and *the* place to come if neither amber nor glitzy alcohol takes your fancy. Their vast array of ceramics, wicker products, glassware, embroidery and lace make ideal souvenirs. Cepelia ⓐ ul. Długa 47 ⓣ 058 301 27 08 ⓦ www.cepelia.pl

TAKING A BREAK

Bar Mleczny Neptun £ ❶ A *bar mleczny* (milk bar), for those who have never experienced it, is a state-subsidised self-service canteen serving up basic, filling fare to the masses for a few złoty. The idea obviously originated in the communist era but has miraculously survived in the face of cut-throat capitalist competition, though the demise of many was inevitable. Choose from the menu on the wall, pay for the food and take your chit to a hatch where you'll either be given your dish immediately, or where you'll wait for a few minutes. Language is obviously an issue here and usually keeps most westerners out (don't expect the 'dinner-ladies' to speak a word of English). The Neptun is the city's most famous milk bar with a typical menu laden with potatoes, meat and cabbage. Long may this institution prosper! ⓐ ul. Długa 33/34 ⓣ 058 301 49 88 ⓒ 07.30–19.00 Mon–Fri, 10.00–18.00 Sat, closed Sun

Café Kamienica £ ❷ One of the best places on one of Poland's prettiest streets, the Kamienica has an easy vibe with a cosy, intimate interior littered with sofas, and outdoor seating, one of the best places to watch the procession of tourists file up Mariacka Street. While away an afternoon with a beer or grab a quick lunch from their range of snacks and soups. ❷ ul. Mariacka 37/39 ❶ 058 301 12 30 ❶ 09.00–23.00

Maraska Tea House & Café £ ❸ Poles are tea-aholics and love nothing better than a great cuppa. It doesn't matter if you are a bean or leaf person here as the tea and coffee are both superb. They claim to stock 120 types of tea and 30 kinds of coffee that can all be sipped in this aromatic little café. It's so popular they have another branch in Gdansk-Wrzeszcz. ❸ ul. Długa 31/32 ❶ 058 301 42 89 ❶ www.maraska.pl ❶ 09.00–18.00

Pierogarnia 'U Dzika' £ ❹ *Dzik* means 'wild boar' in Polish and that's exactly what you'll find minced and filling your *pierogi* at this oddly decorated place in busy Piwna Street (dusty hunting trophies and modern pastel shades – I ask you!). If wild boar doesn't exactly get your juices flowing, you can try fruit, potato, cheese and sauerkraut fillings, but boar is a traditional Gdansk favourite. Despite the naff decor the food is superb, and the outdoor seating has great people-watching potential. ❹ ul. Piwna 59/60 ❶ 058 305 26 76 ❶ 11.00–23.00

Pi Kawa £ ❺ The actual name of this aromatic coffee house is π Kawa. The play on words (or symbols in this case) unfortunately doesn't work in English – π is pronounced 'pi' in

Polish, which almost sounds the same as the word 'drink' and *kawa* means coffee... confused? Open the door of this small place in Piwna Street and immediately all this becomes irrelevant. A simple list of delicious coffees hangs on the wall and the rooms are crammed full of small candlelit tables and young people on dates. A strong coffee aroma perfumes the air. One of the best places in Gdansk for caffeine addicts. Be certain to try the apple pie! ❸ ul. Piwna 5/6 ❶ 058 309 14 44 🕐 10.00–22.00

Schodek £ ❻ This is a cosy place full of sofas and wicker chairs, candles and odd bits of pottery. The coffee is excellent and they serve some of the best cheesecake in town. ❸ ul. Długa 70/71 ❶ 058 301 22 11 Ⓦ www.schodekcafe.pl 🕐 10.00–22.00

Puss & Rose Tea Rooms £–££ ❼ Return to 1930s Sussex at this English-owned tea house where you can drink, or buy loose, some 90 varieties of tea. The confusion of lace and flowery patterns on every conceivable surface represents the very worst of English decor, but they do reportedly make the best hot chocolate in the Tri-City. It's slightly overpriced for true British authenticity. ❸ sw. Ducha 87/89 ❶ 058 301 33 66 🕐 11.00–22.00

AFTER DARK

Restaurants
Rooster £ ❽ Quick, cheap junk food served by sullen waitresses in the Rooster trademark shiny, red hot pants by day,

bar and munchies joint by night. Don't try to chat up the underdressed waitresses – they've heard it all before in slurred English, German and probably Swedish. The crass ranch decor, bedecked with Texas number plates and cowboy hats, completes the tasteless scene. ⓐ ul. Długa 4 ⓣ 058 320 80 93 ⓦ www.rooster.pl ⓛ 11.00–24.00 Sun–Thur, 11.00–01.00 Fri & Sat

Chłopskie Jadło ££ ❾ If it's chunky, filling, full-fat fare you're after to put hairs on your chest on a cold Baltic afternoon, then you could do a lot worse than try some of the dishes on offer at this rural theme restaurant, which also has popular branches in Warsaw and Kraków. Expect lots of hefty timber benches, jars of pickles, ancient agricultural implements and garlands of garlic adorning the bright turquoise walls, as well as a meat-heavy menu. Just a starter and soup will be enough for some. ⓐ ul. Szeroka 33/35 ⓣ 058 301 46 54 ⓦ www.chlopskiejadlo.com.pl ⓛ 12.00–22.00 Mon–Thur, 12.00–24.00 Sat & Sun

Palowa ££ ❿ Another Gdansk institution found deep under the town hall in cellars with stained glass windows, over-attentive waiters and almost theatrically set tables. The Polish cuisine comes in portions as substantial as the stocky dark-wood furniture, and there's a cosy atmosphere despite the size of the place. Great location and definitely sufficient wow-factor for a reasonable price tag. ⓐ ul. Długa 47 ⓣ 058 301 55 32 ⓦ www.palowa.pl ⓛ 11.00–23.00

Piwnica Rajców ££ ⓫ Located deep beneath the Artus Court, this enormous cellar restaurant is good for any occasion – a few drinks at the bar, a quick meal in one of the salons or a full-blown formal dinner in the huge Gothic Hall. The menu has an international flavour with Polish fare sitting side-by-side with South American dishes and exotic seafood. It's one of Poland's best subterranean eateries in one of Gdansk's best locations. Apparently Hitler ate here once; I wonder if he had the Dover sole... ⓐ ul. Długi Targ 44 ⓣ 058 300 02 80 ⓦ www.piwnicarajcow.pl ⓔ pr@piwnicarajcow.pl ⓛ 10.00–23.00

Gdanska £££ ⓬ This Gdansk institution is a vast place that can seat up to 220 people in five halls, each one more elaborately fitted out than the other. Surrounded with so many antiques, paintings, gilt mirrors, Persian rugs and chandeliers, it's like eating in a museum. Though the environment totally distracts from the food, hearty stodgy Polish fare, this is an eatery to bring someone you want to impress with an over-the-top gesture (as the Poles like to do). Whatever you wear, you'll feel underdressed, not that anyone is looking. Go elsewhere for a raucous booze-up. ⓐ ul. Św. Ducha 16/24 ⓣ 058 305 76 71 ⓦ www.gdanska.pl ⓔ restauracja@gdanska.pl ⓛ 12.00–24.00

Bars & clubs

Café Absinthe If you can remember café Absinthe, you weren't there. Sobriety becomes a distant memory as the second glass of the green firewater hits your lips, and the luminous green bar seems to writhe before your eyes. Three absinthes would be nothing short of suicide so retreat to one of the small collection of tables with a glass of tap water and watch the mad alcohol-fuelled night unfurl. Those with facial hair are not recommended to try the 'Flaming Absinthe'. ⓐ ul. Św. Ducha 2 ⓣ 058 320 37 84 ⓛ 10.00–04.00

Miasto Aniołów Situated on Spichlerze Island, the 'City of Angels' is a more grown-up venue that attracts a mid-20s upwards crowd. The music is different every night, there are plenty of seats, and there's even free internet access. During the day, why not try the restaurant, which has a seating area floating on the river. ⓐ ul. Chmielna 26 ⓣ 058 768 58 31 ⓦ www.miastoaniolow.com.pl

Piękni, Młodzi i Bogaci The name of this nightclub means 'beautiful, young and rich', and you'll possibly have to be two of these to even get past the mafia types on the door on busy nights. Inside, the decor is uninspiring and the music is from Poland's Top Ten, but the girls, having taken a few hours off their marketing and management courses, like to come here to let their hair down a bit. ⓐ ul. Teatralna 1 ⓣ 058 305 31 54 ⓦ www.pieknimlodziibogaci.pl ⓛ 21.00–04.00 Wed–Sat

Soda Café Despite its rather innocent name, this club on Spichlerze Island can be pretty hardcore. Upstairs there's an unremarkable restaurant that plays at being something it's not; downstairs a mixed crowd makes the walls and stone-clad bar sweat until dawn. Saturday is erotic night... ⓐ ul. Chmielna 103/104 ⓣ 058 305 12 56 ⓦ www.sodacafe.pl ⓞ 11.00–until last person leaves

Yesterday A friendly hangout in the heart of historical Gdansk for those who are not too choosey about dancing to music their parents probably got on down to. Expect anything from the Beatles to 80s hits downstairs, and a quieter bar area upstairs. A fun place for those who want a less intense night out. ⓐ Piwna 50/51 ⓣ 058 301 39 24 ⓞ 19.00–03.00 Sun–Thur, 19.00–04.00 Fri & Sat

Stare Miasto (Old Town)

Originally a separate settlement, the Old Town is no older than the Main Town and, indeed, many often wrongly refer to the 'Old Town' when they actually mean the Main Town. The Old Town extends north from Podwale Staromiejskie Street to the shipyard and from the railway station to the river. A mix of old and new, this part of town has seen less reconstruction and is altogether less interesting for visitors, though it does have some superior shopping and a couple of sights worth inspecting.

SIGHTS & ATTRACTIONS

Gdansk Shipyard

Though not strictly speaking part of the Old Town, the shipyard can be found to the north, no more than a ten-minute walk from anywhere in the Old Town. Oddly enough, for most westerners this is the most famous place in Gdansk and possibly the only thing the city is known for outside of Poland.

The importance of this place for people now enjoying freedom and democracy from Bohemia to Vladivostok cannot be overstated, as it was here that the communists allowed the first holes in the Soviet dam to go unplugged.

The main draw here is the huge **Monument to Fallen Shipyard Workers**. Unveiled in 1980, it remembers those killed during the strikes of a decade earlier. Three huge 42m- (138ft-) high crosses rise out of the ground bearing anchors, an evocative symbol of the Polish struggle for independence. The

⬥ *Detail from the Monument to Fallen Shipyard Workers*

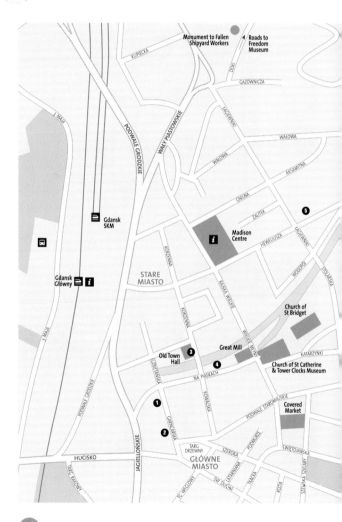

Monument to Fallen
Shipyard Workers

Roads to
Freedom
Museum

KUPIECKA

DOKI

GAZOWNICZA

3 MAJA

PODWALE GRODZKIE

WAŁY PIASTOWSKIE

ŁACHOWNI

WAŁOWA

WAŁOWA

AKSAMITNA

CICHA

ZAUŁEK

Gdansk
SKM

KORZENNA

Madison
Centre

HEWELIUSZA

SOLARSKA

WODOPÓJ

STARE
MIASTO

Gdansk
Główny

KORZENNA

BASZTA WIELKA

Church of
St Bridget

Old Town
Hall

3 MAJA

ELBIETAŃSKA

WIELKIE MŁYNY

Great Mill

KATARZYNKI

Church of St Catherine
& Tower Clocks Museum

NA PIASKACH

KOWALSKA

PODWALE STAROMIEJSKIE

Covered
Market

PODWALE GRODZKIE

JAGIELLOŃSKIE

GARBARSKA

TARG
DRZEWNY

SZEROKA

PODMLKIE

ŚWIĘTOJAŃSKA

HUCISKO

TARG RAKOWY

GŁÓWNE
MIASTO

SW. DUCHA

TACKA

KOZA

TG. WĘGLOWY

 LAWENDOWA

ARTUSZ

PIWNA

MARIACKA

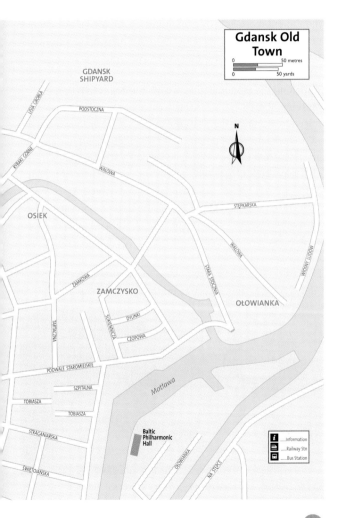

monument represents the communist regime's first admittance of wrongdoing and is, therefore, the starting point in a story that ended with the fall of the Berlin Wall, a section of which stands nearby.

Behind the monument don't miss the **Roads to Freedom Museum** housed in the BHP Hall where the communists were forced to recognise the existence of the Solidarity Movement in 1981. Black-and-white photos, news clippings, recordings and artefacts from the period tell the Solidarity story in a very effective way. For those who never experienced the Eastern Bloc or the period immediately after its collapse, some of the exhibits give a brief taste of what life was like in a communist state. Highlights include a mock-up of a communist era grocer's shop, a bust of Lenin and footage from the period Poland spent under martial law in the early 1980s.

ⓐ ul. Doki 1 ☏ 058 308 47 12 ⓦ www.fcs.org.pl ⌚ 10.00–17.00 Tues–Sun, May–Sept; 10.00–16.00 Tues–Sun, Oct–Apr

◯ *The Solidarity banner adorns the gates of Gdansk Shipyard*

⬥ *A battered section of the Berlin Wall*

Great Mill

The bizarre building of the Great Mill opposite the Church of St Catherine was built in the mid-14th century by the Teutonic Knights and was the largest mill in Europe for many centuries. Only the bombs of World War II halted the machinery inside. Rebuilt in the 1960s, its giant slanting roof now covers a shopping mall (see page 26), though some of the old machinery is exhibited inside.

The Old Town's churches

Back in the Old Town proper, two churches stand out among the crowd. The **Church of St Catherine** *was* one of the finest in Gdansk and the oldest. It was partially burnt down in May of 2006 and is yet to reopen. When it does, the main focus of interest here will once again be the grave of astronomer

THE FIGHT FOR DEMOCRACY

It was here at the Gdansk shipyard that manual workers were killed during the strikes in 1970, and where, a decade later, the Solidarity Movement (see page 17) was founded by a shipyard electrician called Lech Wałęsa. He secured substantial political and social concessions from the Polish government in 1980 but the year after, his Solidarity trade union was outlawed, and Wałęsa imprisoned. After being released in 1982, Wałęsa was awarded the Nobel Peace Prize in 1983, and, after organising more crippling strikes in 1988, was elected President in 1990 – a term that was to last for five years.

Johannes Hevelius, an erstwhile inhabitant of the city who is buried in the choir. Next door the **Church of St Bridget** is also worthy of a peek inside. Only rebuilt in the 1970s it was a place

⬤ *The tranquil surrounds of St Catherine's Church*

of worship adopted by Lech Wałęsa and Solidarity in the 1980s. Away from all the Solidarity imagery, the most interesting feature here is the as yet unfinished amber altar. When complete it will contain 6.5 tons of the prehistoric resin!

Old Town Hall

Worth a gaze skywards, if you happen to find yourself in Korzenna Street near the Great Mill, is the Old Town Hall dating from the Renaissance period. It was used as the Red Army headquarters after World War II as it miraculously escaped the bombardment intact, and is one of only a handful of original structures in the city centre. The interior is open to the public and contains: a grand hall where concerts take place, a bookshop, the Baltic Sea Cultural Centre, and a restaurant in the cellar.

CULTURE

Tower Clocks Museum

While at the Church of St Catherine, pop in to see this small museum of old tower clocks dating from the 15th to the 19th centuries.

ⓐ ul. Wielkie Młyny 🕐 10.00–17.00 Tues–Sun

RETAIL THERAPY

Covered Market It cost 20 million złoty to renovate this neo-Gothic building, and during the work the JCBs hit on the foundations of one of Gdansk's oldest recorded churches. Even if you haven't come to buy anything from the stalls laden with dairy and meat products, Vietnamese clothing and other assorted tack, you can still take a look at the bits of archaeology in the basement. ⓐ ul. Pańska ⓛ 09.00–19.00 Mon–Fri, 09.00–17.00 Sat, 10.00–15.00 Sun

Great Mill Shopping Centre Worth a visit just to see the inside of the Great Mill (see page 26). ⓐ Wielkie Młyny 16 ⓣ 058 301 10 31 ⓛ 11.00–19.00 Mon–Fri, 11.00–15.00 Sat

Madison Centre The glass and steel presence of the Madison Centre means that city-breakers can get their fix of mall-style shopping a few hundred metres from the historical centre. There are almost 100 shops including many of the well-known outlets you love so much on the high street or in the mall back home, and many Polish ones you've never heard of (and never will again). There's also a gym, a tourist information point, underground parking, a children's playground and a host of squeaky-clean, faceless eateries. ⓐ ul. Rajska 10 ⓣ 058 766 75 35 ⓦ www.madison.gda.pl ⓔ info@madison.gda.pl ⓛ 09.00–21.00 Mon–Sat, 10.00–20.00 Sun

TAKING A BREAK

Green Way £ ❶ This is a minimalist veggie diner near the railway station – a sort of Ryanair of vegetarian restaurants (though with friendlier staff). It's too bright, the food is cheap and the environment sterile, but you can be sure nothing's contaminated with meat. Second branch in the Main Town

(ul. Długa 11). ⓐ ul. Garncarska 4/6 ⓣ 058 301 41 21
ⓛ 10.00–20.00 Mon–Fri, 12.00–20.00 Sat & Sun

Puerto Coffee Culture £ ❷ Puerto stock an unbelievable variety
of coffee and fans of the bean will be in caffeine heaven before
long. A clean-cut, stylish place with a relaxed, welcoming
atmosphere that gets rave reviews, especially for its live music.
ⓐ ul. Garncarska 7/9 ⓣ 058 305 55 98 ⓦ www.puerto.pl
ⓛ 11.00–23.00

AFTER DARK

Irish Pub £ ❸ Did you come all this way to drink Guinness and
watch Sky Sports? Well, if you did, this is the place to come. They
regularly hold wild events and live music concerts down in the
sweaty cellars of the Old Town Hall. ⓐ ul. Korzenna 33/35
ⓣ 058 320 24 74 ⓦ www.irish.pl ⓛ 15.00–04.00

Gospoda Pod Wielkim Młynem £–££ ❹ The 'Pub under the
Great Mill' has probably the best beer garden in town,
surrounded as it is by willow trees dipping their branches into
the Radunia Canal, which flows on either side. Just don't get so
drunk that you forget that you're surrounded by water. The
Polish food is OK, but it's best to come here on a warm
summer's evening for few pints of *piwo* in the garden. ⓐ ul. Na
Piaskach 1 ⓣ 058 302 17 79 ⓛ 12.00–21.00

Swojski smak £–££ ❺ The name of this eatery translates as
'Our Taste' and has a firm focus on simple, hearty Polish dishes

to beef you up against the Baltic breeze. The mammoth country portions they dish up here are excellent value and the kitschy faux-rural theme doesn't distract too much. I wonder what 'soup prepared according to the fantasy of the day' tastes like? There's a second branch in Gdynia. ⓐ ul. Heweliusza 25/27 ⓣ 058 320 19 12 ⓦ www.swojskismak.pl ⓔ restauracja@swojskismak.pl ⓛ 12.00–22.00 Mon–Fri, 13.00–22.00 Sat & Sun

Outside the Centre

Beyond the confines of the Main and Old Towns, Gdansk has
several interesting and historically significant sights to enjoy.
The two main areas are the port, which witnessed the first
salvos of World War II, and the district of Oliwa with its
cathedral and park. None of the following are particularly
difficult to reach by public transport.

SIGHTS & ATTRACTIONS

Lighthouse

The unassuming Gdansk lighthouse near the Stockhom ferry
terminal has had a more turbid history than you might imagine.
Dating from 1894, its design was based on the Cleveland Main
Lighthouse in the US. Until 1939 it served a triple purpose as a
coastal lighthouse, a harbour pilots' tower and a time ball
station. On the day the Nazis attacked Poland in September
1939, the first rounds of World War II were fired from a window

HAVE YOU SEEN THIS GUN?

The owner of the lighthouse is looking to fit a new time
ball to the top and is also trying to trace the gun that fired
the first shots of the war. It was captured by the British as
a war trophy, but then the trail goes cold. If anyone knows
where it is, the lighthouse keeper would like it back, please,
so he can mount it outside the lighthouse for all to
admire.

◯ *The unusual exterior of Oliwa Cathedral*

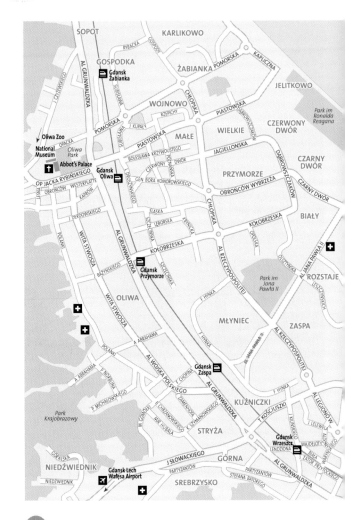

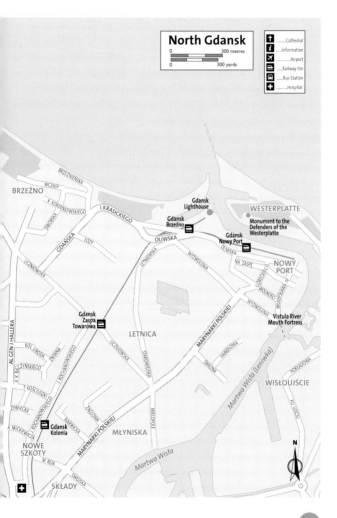

North Gdansk

0   300 metres
0   300 yards

↑ ....Cathedral
𝒊 ....Information
✈ ....Airport
🚆 ....Railway Stn
🚌 ....Bus Station
✚ ....Hospital

BRZEŹNIENSKA
WCZASY
BRZEŹNO
K. KORZENIOWSKIEGO
I KRASICKIEGO
DROBISKA
GDANSKA
ŁOZY
OLIWSKA
Gdansk Lighthouse
Gdansk Brzeźno
WESTERPLATTE
Monument to the Defenders of the Westerplatte
Gdansk Nowy Port
OLIWSKA
NA ZASPĘ
NOWY PORT
UCZNIOWSKA
LETNICKA
WYZWOLENIA
GÓRECKIEGO
WOLNOŚCI
WYZWOLENIA
WŁADYSŁAWA IV
Vistula River Mouth Fortress
Gdansk Zaspa Towarowa
LETNICA
UCZNIOWSKA
STAROWIEJSKA
MARYNARKI POLSKIEJ
HANDLOWA
POKŁADOWA
WISŁOUJSCIE
AL GEN J HALLERA
KOL URODA
IWIANA
K K BA
CZYNSKIEGO
T KOSCIUSKI O
ŁOCHANOWSKIEGO
ŻWIRKEJA
ŻAGLOWA
NARWICKA
MARYNARKI POLSKIEJ
WIELOPOLE
ŚNILOWA
Martwa Wisła (Leniwka)
PL USCI
Gdansk Kolonia
MŁYNISKA
A MICKIEWICZA
NOWE SZKOTY
M REJA
SKŁADY
SWOJSKA
Martwa Wisła

N

93

halfway up and aimed at the Polish garrison on the Westerplatte across the river. The Poles returned fire, taking out the gun and damaging the lighthouse, and the bullet holes and mangled bits of iron can still be seen today. Bought by a Pole who emigrated to Germany in the 1960s, the lighthouse was renovated and opened for the public who can now climb to the top for great views of the port area.

ⓐ ul. Przemyslowa 6a ⓣ 058 760 16 42 ⓦ www.lighthouse.pl ⓛ 10.00–19.00 Mon–Sun, June–Sept ⓝ Tram: 13

Oliwa Cathedral

The leafy old residential district of Oliwa is situated 7 km (4^1/$_2$ miles) to the northwest of the Main Town and is a magnet for visitors looking for a relaxing few hours of unchallenging sightseeing and perhaps a picnic in the park. It's one of Gdansk's more prestigious postcodes, and even Lech Wałęsa keeps a villa somewhere in the tree-lined avenues. Oliwa dates back to AD 1186 when the Cistercian order founded a monastery there. The cathedral was begun in 1178, but is a real hotchpotch of styles with a baroque entrance way seemingly jammed between two red-brick octagonal Renaissance towers, and a lofty Gothic interior, making it one of the most peculiar-looking cathedrals you may ever see. It's the longest church in Poland and only suffered minor damage in World War II. The highlight of the interior is the rococo organ with 7,896 pipes and decorated with trumpet-playing angels, which is used to give year-round, free organ concerts here (check with the tourist office back in Gdansk for schedules). The acoustics are incredible.

● *Oliwa Park is a favourite spot for locals to relax*

Oliwa Park

Everyone calls this Oliwa Park, but the official name for this piece of welcome greenery is the Adam Mickiewicz Park. The lawns of the larger English-style part are littered with pieces of modern sculpture and ancient trees, whereas the French-style stretch is a more formal affair. Within the park you will also find the Abbot's Palace (now a modern art gallery) and a hothouse. Nearby is Oliwa Zoo (see page 134).

Westerplatte

The Westerplatte is a chunk of land at the mouth of Gdansk's harbour which, between the wars, was Polish territory (as opposed to Gdansk itself which was the Free City). In 1939 it went down in history as the place where World War II began its long and bloody narrative when the Nazi ship, the *Schleswig-Holstein*, and soldiers positioned in the lighthouse on the opposite bank of the river, opened fire on the Polish garrison at dawn on 1 September 1939. The garrison held out for another 7 days with just 180 men. The main attraction here is the **Monument to the Defenders of the Westerplatte**, which commemorates that valiant act. This monolithic piece of socialist realism stands on raised ground overlooking the harbour entrance. The only other places of interest are some of the original ruins and Guardhouse No. 1, which contains a small exhibition on the battle. It's only worth the trip if you have a particular interest in World War II history, or are spending a longer period of time in the Tri-City.

Ⓝ Bus: 106, boat from Gdansk waterfront

⬤ *The Abbot's Palace at Oliwa is now a modern art gallery*

CULTURE

Ethnographic Museum

Located opposite the Bishop's Palace in Oliwa Park, this small museum houses a collection of furniture, fishing tools, agricultural implements and handicrafts from the Kashubian region to the southwest of Gdansk.

ⓐ ul. Cystersów 19 **ⓣ** 058 552 41 39 **ⓛ** 09.00–16.00 Tues–Fri, 10.00–16.00 Sat & Sun, Oct–May; 09.00–16.00 Tues–Fri , 10.00–17.00 Sat & Sun, June–Sept

National Museum

The National Museum's main building, a former Franciscan monastery, stands in the midst of the rarely visited Old Suburb (Stare Przedmieście) to the south of the Main Town. Packed full of Gothic art as well as some works by Dutch masters, the most celebrated exhibit is Hans Memling's painting, *The Last Judgement*.

ⓐ ul. Toruńska 1 **ⓣ** 058 301 70 61
ⓦ www.muzeum.narodowe.gda.pl **ⓛ** 09.00–16.00 Tues–Fri, 10.00–16.00 Sat & Sun **ⓝ** Bus: 121

RETAIL THERAPY

Apart from a few forlorn souvenir stands, there's not much in the way of consumer capitalism at Gdansk's far-flung sights. Give the credit card a day off and leave your złoty lining your wallet for later.

⬤ *Autumn colours, countryside around Gdansk*

TAKING A BREAK

Oliwa Park is the one of the best places in the Tri-City to recover from temple fatigue. Pack a picnic and spend a lazy afternoon watching the daisies grow. The riverbanks around the Westerplatte and the lighthouse have also seen a few cafés and snack bars sprout up in the last few years.

AFTER DARK

None of the above are places you'd particularly wish to be after dark (especially the port area). The vast majority of people, after a day's sightseeing outside of the confines of Gdansk's Main Town, scurry back to the familiarity of western hotels and comfortingly overpriced restaurants on the city's touristy thoroughfares.

▶ *Fishing boats on the Baltic Sea coast*

Sopot

The small seaside resort of Sopot has something for all visitors looking for a good time by the Baltic on long summer days and nights. The beach, pier and nightclubs lining the coast combine to provide a seaside experience unique in the region and seem to attract half of Poland's plain dwellers during the holiday months as well as a large contingent of foreigners, mostly from Germany. The fashionable boutiques, street cafés and well-dressed visitors create a wholly different atmosphere from its Tri-City comrades, and Sopot feels a million miles away from dreary Gdynia and lofty Gdansk. Thanks to its popularity, even among Polish celebrities, it's also one of the most expensive and exclusive places to live and stay in the country. If Sopot was the only place you visited, you'd get a pretty warped view of what life is really like in Poland.

SPA WITH THE FAMOUS

For centuries a tiny fishing village, Sopot became popular as a spa town in the 19th century. The spa was initially set up in 1823 by Jean Georg Haffner, a surgeon in Napoleon's army, who also had the first pier built. Sopot grew even trendier in the 1920s and 1930s as it became a place where the rich and famous came to see and be seen. A long list of illustrious and infamous visitors to Sopot include Adolf Hitler, Fidel Castro, Marlena Dietrich and Omar Sharif, so you're in good company.

GETTING THERE

The easiest way to reach Sopot is by taking the SKM commuter train from Gdansk Main Railway Station. The journey takes around 25 minutes and costs a few złoty. You can also take the 'water tram' to and from Gdansk and Hel; it's a much more expensive way to travel, but the journey is considerably more interesting.

SIGHTS & ATTRACTIONS

Aquapark

After splashing the day away in one of the many pools (see page 133), including a year-round outdoor pool, relax in the sauna and then sup away the evening at the bar and restaurant.

ⓐ ul. Zamkowa Góra 3/5 ☎ 058 555 85 55

ⓦ www.aquaparksopot.pl ⓔ info@aquaparksopot.pl

🕙 08.00–22.00 Sept–June; 08.30–22.30 July & Aug

Bohaterów Monte Cassino Street

Life in the centre of Sopot very much revolves around the wide main drag, which runs from the Church of St George at the top down to the pier. The long name means 'Heroes of Monte Cassino Street' and commemorates the part Polish troops played at the Battle of Monte Cassino during World War II. Its length is lined with glittering shopfronts, street cafés, banks, galleries, theatres, cinemas, ice cream parlours and one bold chunk of contemporary architecture (see Krzywy Dom, page 114). The pedestrian zone is a cool place to stroll with a date, sip a coffee, have a meal and empty your bank account.

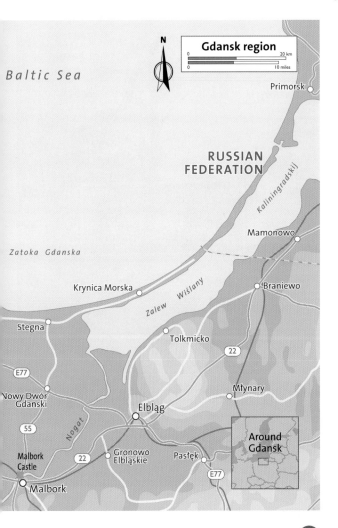

▲ The road to Hel

Gdynia & Hel

If the towns that make up the Tri-City were three girlie mates in a club, Gdansk would be the popular one with the looks, Sopot would attract suitors with her bubbly personality, but Gdynia would be the dull one hoping to pick up scraps from the others. Without the other two, the modern port to the north of Sopot would hardly ever get a mention in any guidebook, despite the best efforts of the tourist authorities to promote it as an up-and-coming place. It isn't, but there is some reasonable mall shopping for those that way inclined.

Passing quickly through Gdynia you find yourself on the Hel Peninsula, a thin strip of sand hardly wide enough in some places to accommodate the road and rail track that run its length, in others substantial enough to support a small town. Stop anywhere and you're sure to find a sandy beach a few hundred metres both north and south. At the tip of the sandbar is the tiny town of Hel, a former military zone with barrack-like blocks of flats, a few half-timbered fishermen's cottages and a couple of tourist facilities. Most people either come here to tell their mates they've been to Hel and back, end up here because they can't go any further otherwise they'd end up in the Baltic, or come to visit the wonderful *Fokarium*, a small seal sanctuary containing up to ten grey seals and well worth seeing (just don't feed them any coins!).

Trains run from Gdansk's Main Railway Station to Hel (though not very often) but you can always take a short-cut by going by boat (the water tram as the locals insist on calling it) which leaves Gdansk four times a day in summer from near the Fish Market. The boat journey provides an excellent opportunity

🔺 *Resident of the* Fokarium, *Hel*

to glimpse some of the sights in the port area such as the lighthouse and the Westerplatte, as well as the beaches, piers and villages lining the Bay of Gdansk.

Sopot beach

In the summer heat, Sopot's long, parkland-backed stretch of sand is the place to be. Waves break onto a broad stretch of warm, soft, white sand before sliding back into the Baltic, and when the sun comes out and the temperature tips over the 20°C (68°F) mark, the shoreline fills up with slowly roasting Poles. Slap on the factor 15 and join them. There are bathing huts and deckchairs for hire for the sedate, while the more energetic might be out for a morning constitutional walk, jog, power-walk or bike ride along a track that runs all the way back to Gdansk. The average summer day on Sopot beach is a bit like

◆ *Promenading on Sopot Pier*

being at a British seaside resort – people enjoy the sand, but the water is there just for show and to provide background noise. On very hot days some do venture into the waters of the Baltic Sea, though generally this is avoided for obvious reasons. The water is at its 'warmest' in late August and early September.

In winter the beach becomes a place for brisk walks in the cold, invigorating air, laden with microelements so good for the lungs. The beach is likely to be deserted any other time than summer, which also has its charms.

On balmy summer evenings the sand jigs to the disco beat emitted from the line of clubs along the shoreline. Drinking, smooching, barbecuing and general frivolity normally go on into the wee hours here. Amazingly, despite the various activities the nightclubs bring to the beach, it's a very clean stretch of sand without a plastic bottle (or worse) in sight.

Sopot Pier

As every Tri-City resident will no doubt have you promptly know, the wooden pier in Sopot is the longest in the universe (or Europe depending on who you ask). It comes as little surprise, therefore, that Sopot is twinned with the English seaside resort of Southend-on-Sea; obviously the length of their respective piers being the common denominator (if precious little else). However, Southend's pier at over 1.6 km (1 mile) long beats Sopot's hands down; Sopot's manages just 500 m (1,640 ft) but is, after all, made of wood. Its timber stilts were rammed into the sand in the early 19th century, but it was always packed away for winter. A permanent structure appeared in the early

20th century, but has been swept away by storms several times, most recently in 2004. There are various tacky attractions along its length, and when the tourist crowds are out promenading, there's an admission fee to get on.

CULTURE

Opera Leśna (Forest Opera)

As far as culture in Sopot goes, the Opera Leśna (Forest Opera) has little to rival it. Formed from the natural contours of the land like a natural amphitheatre in the forest (to the west of the railway station), it can seat 4,200 people. Despite its name, it isn't just opera you can see there, and in fact the main event to take place there every year in August is the Sopot International Song Contest.

> **BIGGER THAN EUROVISION?**
> Very often compared to the Eurovision Song Contest, the Sopot International Song Contest has been running since 1961. Now half contest, half megaconcert, big names to have appeared at the show in recent years include Elton John, Whitney Houston, Simply Red, Bryan Adams, The Corrs, Annie Lennox, Vanessa Mae and Katie Melua (who absolutely everyone in Poland thinks is English). This list of illustriati hints at the significance of the event and its dissimilarity to Eurovision! Another glaring difference is that in 2006 it was Britain that won the competition section with alternative hip hop duo Mattafix (who?). Hip hop is still big in Poland.

RETAIL THERAPY

Bohaterów Monte Cassino Street is the only place to spend your wads of złoty or ruin your credit rating. Designer labels, pricey antiques, original artwork and local handicrafts are what most people find themselves taking home.

TAKING A BREAK

Extending for 10 km (6 miles) from just to the north of Sopot all the way to Gdansk, a coast-hugging cycle path offers a great way to escape from the crowds of both places. There are several bike-hire places in Sopot. The beach is the obvious place to loaf and laze unless there's not a square inch left for your beach towel. Usually a short walk in either direction sees the crowds thin out.

Bar Elita £ Escape the tourists and eat with the Poles at this low-cost pub serving well-prepared Polish staples with a smile. ⓐ ul. Podjazd 3 ❶ 058 551 06 20 ❶ 09.00–23.00

Bar Przystań £ If you only visit one fish restaurant in the Tri-City, or Poland for that matter, this should be it. A no-nonsense place that concentrates on food rather than fancy decor. Choose from a huge selection of seafood dishes and enjoy it inside or out on the terrace overlooking the sea where the food was probably swimming around the day before. Avoid the more exotic dishes such as shark, and go for fresher local fare instead. Prices here are pleasantly low. ⓐ al. Wojska Polskiego 11 ❶ 058 555 06 61 ⓦ www.barprzystan.pl ❶ 11.00–23.00

◔ Meet the Sopot locals

Café Zaścianek £ Away from the parasols and false smiles on Sopot's main thoroughfare, the Zaścianek is a cosy little oasis of authenticity tucked away in a side street off Bohaterów Monte Cassino. Small, intimate tables, shimmering candlelight and a more tranquil vibe make this the ideal venue for arty talk and travellers' tales. Your visit may even coincide with a chamber concert or a poetry reading. ⓐ ul. Haffnera 3/1A ⓣ 058 550 05 43 ⓛ 11.00–22.00 Sun–Thur, 11.00–23.00 Fri & Sat

Kawiarnia u Hrabiego £ Another hideaway from the holiday crowds and a place that evokes the 19th-century atmosphere of the spa town Sopot once was. Creaky floors, net curtains, tinkling tea trays and heaps of old-world charm provide a let-up from the in-your-face plasticky café scene in more frequented parts of town. The building also houses the office of the Friends of Sopot Society who organise concerts and exhibitions there. ⓐ ul. Czyżewskiego 12 ⓣ 058 551 07 56 ⓦ www.dworek.art.pl ⓛ 10.00–22.00 Mon–Sun

Krzywy Dom £-££ Officially called the Rezydent Shopping Centre (though absolutely no-one uses the name) the Krzywy Dom (Crooked House) is a typical piece of zany post-communist architecture, probably designed by someone who criticised the communists for 40 years for building monstrosities. While it could be seen as just a bit of fun, it sits badly among the other 19th-century buildings in Bohaterów Monte Cassino Street and looks a bit like a normal house viewed through the bottom of a bottle. Inside there are more cafés, restaurants and pubs pretending to be older, than you can shake a stick at. The other advantage of being inside is that it's the one place in the street where you can't see the outside. ⓐ ul. Haffnera 6 ① 058 555 52 00 ⓛ opening hours differ for each café/restaurant in the centre.

AFTER DARK

Nightclubs & pubs

Atelier This is a really laid back nightspot with a great location right on the beach. Thursday's sounds are groove and funky, Friday is 70s and 80s night and Saturday is a blend of pop, rock and dance. The parties here often continue well past sunrise and the terrace is a superb place to watch the sun come up over the Baltic. Can be a touch pricier than other clubs.
ⓐ al. Mamuszki 2 ① 058 555 89 06 ⓦ www.klubatelier.pl
ⓔ klubatelier@wp.pl ⓛ 15.00–until last person leaves Mon–Fri, 11.00–until last person leaves Sat & Sun

Club Mandarynka If you're into sharp suits and girls dressed to kill, this trendy, contemporary, retro hangout is Sopot's last word in late-night sophistication. The superbly designed interior with flamingo-pink sofas, pink leather bar stools and countless pieces of 60s and 70s retro furniture fills at the weekend with clubbers out to party hard after a week closing deals on their mobile phones. Attracts a few moody mafia types, and you're more likely to get in on busy nights if you look as though you carry a gun or have a foreign passport. ⓐ ul. Bema 6 ① 058 550 45 63
ⓦ www.mandarynka.pl ⓔ mandarynka@mandarynka.pl
ⓛ 11.30–until last person leaves Mon–Sun

Club 70 One of Sopot's less self-obsessed and more enjoyable late-night venues. Borrow your baby-booming parents' glad rags and join the medallion-toting cool dudes in their Cuban-heels and chicks in their bangles and bell-bottom jumpsuits to travel back in time to the summer of '76. Housed in a cellar in Sopot's main street. ⓐ ul. Bohaterów Monte Cassino 60 ⓣ 058 550 77 77 ⓦ www.club70.pl ⓛ 12.00–02.00 Mon–Thur, 12.00–06.00 Fri & Sat

Karczma Irena A great little pub and restaurant with an authentic rural Kashubian theme. Chunky rural timber tables creak under generous portions of hearty Polish fare, and the beer's good too. You may even be lucky enough to catch a performance of local traditional music. ⓐ ul. Chopina 36 ⓣ 058 551 20 73 ⓛ 13.00–24.00

Koliba Koliba (which means mountain chalet) is something of a shock when you first walk through the door. The last thing you expect on the Baltic coast is an oversized log cabin from the Tatra Mountains full of partygoers. The chunky timber tables surround the tiny dance floor in front of the bar, but usually the party spills out onto the beach. It's an odd place where you can come to warm your insides with some tea and rum on a cold winter's day or enjoy a hot night out in the summer months with cocktails and dancing. ⓐ ul. Powstańców Warszawy 90 (Park Północny) ⓣ 050 135 96 98 ⓦ www.koliba.pl ⓔ adam@koliba.pl ⓛ 09.00–01.00 Sun–Tues, 09.00–05.00 Wed–Sat

Papryka Papryka's owners must have bought up Poland's red paint surplus to decorate this hot place. Scarlet walls, cherry chairs, rosy lanterns and crimson sofas can be found in several red rooms in a villa near the pier. Funk and house are the orders of the day here with the occasional live performance.
ⓐ ul.Grunwaldzka 11 (Łazienki Południowe) ① 058 551 74 76
ⓦ www.klubpapryka.pl ⓔ info@klubpapryka.pl ① 15.00—until last person leaves Mon–Sun

Plaża Piratów Another place on the beach, this time with a strong maritime theme. It's more of a pub/bar/restaurant than other places in the neighbourhood and completely open to the night air in summer. There's excellent food and beer on offer and ask to try the speciality of the house – lime and coffee granules washed down with a shot of rum. You could also have a pillow fight with a mate on the yard arm in front of the bar with the whole place looking on in bemusement. ⓐ Łazienki Północne, wejście nr 14 ① 058 555 30 31 ⓦ www.plazapiratow.pl
ⓔ tawerna@plazapiratow.pl ① 10.00–23.00 Mon–Sun

Rooster Part of a chain with branches across Poland and frequented by males who come to gawp at the waitresses in the tightest shiny, red hot pants you're likely to see in a public place. It's a decent, no-nonsense locale in which to down a few glasses of Żubrówka and apple juice, and if you get the munchies their junk food menu will do the trick. Otherwise it's a pretty predictable joint. ⓐ ul. Bohaterów Monte Cassino 54
① 058 550 74 04 ⓦ www.rooster.pl/sopot ⓔ sopot@rooster.pl
① 11.00–24.00 Sun–Thur, 11.00–01.00 Fri & Sat

Spatif Spatif hides itself away up a staircase above the Rooster Pub. Ring the bell at the top, and try to persuade the bruiser on the door to let you in. Speaking English helps but this is one of the most difficult places to enter. Inside you'll find a real exclusive arty hideaway and one of the best (and smallest) clubs in town. The Persian carpets, artwork on the walls and ornate sofas create a real Bohemian vibe. Live jazz sessions are a regular feature. ⓐ ul. Bohaterów Monte Cassino 54 ⓣ 058 550 26 83 ⓦ www.spatif.sopot.pl ⓔ spatif@sopot.pl ⓛ 15.00–until last person leaves Mon–Sun

Viva Club Heralded as the No. 1 club in the Tri-City, Viva is certainly one of the best nights out in the area. There are two dance floors and various bars scattered around the place, and from Wednesday to Sunday morning the fun never stops. Top DJs from around Europe and some completely unhinged events make this one of the best places to head for. Dance till your legs are about to fall off then bail out to chill out on the beach. ⓐ al. Mamuszki 2 ⓣ 058 551 53 23 ⓦ www.vivaclub.pl ⓔ viva@vivaclub.pl ⓛ 21.00–until last person leaves Thur–Sat

ACCOMMODATION

Pension Eden £ Possibly the best of the budget bunch with basic but comfortable rooms, modern bathrooms and one or two reminders that this is one of the oldest hotels in Sopot. Good value for money and centrally located. ⓐ ul. Księdza Kordeckiego 4/6 ⓣ 058 551 15 03 ⓦ www.hotel-eden.pl ⓔ edensopot@hotel-eden.pl

Willa Marea ££ With 15 light, airy, classy rooms, this is Sopot's only real boutique hotel. Situated next to the beach there are great sea views from some of the rooms. The staff are extremely accommodating, lots of free extras are thrown in and the location is superb. ⓐ ul. Chrobrego 38 ⓣ 058 555 84 80 ⓕ 058 555 84 81 ⓦ www.marea.sopot.pl ⓔ rezerwacje@marea.sopot.pl

Grand Hotel £££ Built in the confident, sweeping style of the 1920s, the Grand was the only proper hotel in the golden age of stylish interwar travel. Only the very rich could grace its corridors, and the casino next door relieved them of so much money it was actually an important source of municipal revenue for the Free City before the war. It may have lost a touch of its opulence inside since then, though the 127 air-conditioned rooms are extremely stylish and comfortable, but from the outside the building still makes a grand statement as it dominates the shoreline. For some reason the hotel website fails to mention that Hitler occupied rooms 221–3 immediately after doing the same to Poland. ⓐ ul. Powstańców Warszawy 12/14 ⓣ 058 520 60 00 ⓕ 058 520 60 99 ⓦ www.orbis.pl ⓔ sof.grand.sopot@orbis.pl

Malbork

Malbork is an unremarkable small rural town on the River Nogat, to which the vast majority of visitors to the region would not give a second glance, were it not for the colossal red-brick Gothic castle complex to the northwest of the small centre, built by the Teutonic Knights in the late 13th century. Malbork Castle is one of Poland's top tourist sights on merit and makes a great, must-see day trip for those spending more than a few days in the Tri-City area.

The castle has an oversize history to match its bulky ramparts. As mentioned, it was founded by the Teutonic Knights as the centre of their order when they were forced out of Palestine. Over two centuries they added more and more buildings making it into the mountain of bricks we see today. The knights only used Malbork as their capital for 200 years before being forced to sell the castle to the Czechs due to financial problems. The crafty Czechs sold it on to the Polish king for a hefty profit. Subsequent Polish monarchs stayed here for three centuries when on their tax-collecting missions from Warsaw to Gdansk, before the Prussians moved in following the partition of Poland in the late 18th century. Given a neo-Gothic makeover in the 19th century, it was used as a POW camp for commonwealth soldiers by the Nazis until 1945, when the Red Army reduced over half of the buildings to rubble. The site was left to the elements and looters until 1961 when the Malbork Castle Museum was established. Much has been rebuilt, and the castle is now a UNESCO-protected site. The red-brick ramparts and courtyards provide a perfect backdrop for film crews and many a Polish and German film has been shot here.

As one of the country's prime destinations, it attracts swarms of tourists in summer, made up in part by hordes of German tour bus retirees who shuffle, in a painfully slow way, through the huge fortress. Add to that thousands of bored Polish school kids on epic three-hour tours, agitated guides and a confusing maze of medieval corridors and passageways and the mass tourism scene is complete. To avoid the crowds you could join a Polish tour and try to slip away to explore yourself, but you risk getting lost and coming across many locked doors. The best way to see the castle is to hire a private guide just for yourself and put a time limit on the tour of, say, 90 minutes.

● *The imposing form of Malbork Castle*

GETTING THERE

Malbork straddles the Gdansk–Warsaw mainline and many express and local trains make the one hour- to 90 minutes-long journey from Gdansk. There are also regular buses to and from Gdansk. The bus and train stations are situated next to one another ten minutes' walk southeast of the castle.

● *The Gothic splendour of Malbork Castle gable*

SIGHTS & ATTRACTIONS

The Castle

Having bought a ticket, joined a group and made it over the first drawbridge across the moat, you find yourself in the large courtyard of the **Middle Castle**, an original structure built by the Teutonic Knights when they moved their nerve centre to Malbork. To the right is the **Grand Masters' Palace** and to the left several renovated spaces house exhibitions. The most impressive of these must be the Amber Museum, where you can gaze at amazing collections of jewellery, altars, sculptures and other objects crafted from 'Baltic Gold'. Another interesting exhibition is the mock-up of the castle kitchen where you can feel the heat of the huge stoves and smell the food that would have been prepared there.

Moving on from the Middle Castle, another drawbridge under a portcullis leads to the smaller courtyard of the **High Castle**, the oldest part of the fortress. Climbing the steps to the first floor balcony you find the Chapter House with its amazing floor and Gothic frescoes, the Treasury where amber was kept

CONVENIENT SIGNPOSTS

Look out for the small plaques around the castle with small devils in various positions. These are actually signposts to the many toilets the castle once had. A devil with crossed legs and spread wings meant that the nearest convenience was a long way away, and his beard indicated the direction to the nearest hole in the ramparts.

and rooms belonging to important dignitaries in the order. The tour then usually continues into the **Church of Our Lady**, which is still undergoing restoration. From the state of the place it looks like this will be the case for many decades to come, as little remains of the pre-1945 building. The façade once held a huge statue of the Virgin Mary, but this was destroyed by Soviet shells at the end of the war. The last remaining highlight is the **Main Tower**, which, for an extra fee, can be climbed to admire the views of the surrounding countryside.

There are many other rooms and features too numerous to mention here. Whether you see everything depends on the time you give yourself. If it all gets too much inside the castle, you can always take a break in one of the courtyards.

RETAIL THERAPY

Unless you really just can't say goodbye to Poland's shores without an imitation Teutonic knight's sword, a kitsch figure of a chain-mailed warrior, a made-in-China t-shirt sporting a crusader's cross or some fake amber, forget shopping here. What you can't buy in Gdansk, you certainly won't find in Malbork.

TAKING A BREAK

Malbork heaves with tourists even on winter Wednesdays, and all those hordes of German tour bus zombies discovering their history can be too much even for seasoned travellers. Miraculously, just across the wide River Nogat you'll find only a handful of tourists intrepid enough to have headed out of sight of their coaches. Cross the wooden footbridge by the Piwniczka restaurant to the other bank from which you'll get the best snaps of the castle in its entirety. The best shot can be taken late in the day when the setting sun turns the red bricks a fiery orange.

Grabbing a coffee or a bite to eat is a matter of just choosing at random which snack kiosk or tent to enter. There are considerably more of these in summer than in winter. Prices are high by Polish standards, as you would expect at one of the country's top tourist attractions.

🔺 *Malbork town itself is refreshingly crowd free*

AFTER DARK

Pub Baszta £ ❶ Taking up three floors of the former southern gate into the town, near the river south of the castle, this is a rowdy, rural place and an interesting watering hole where you can down a few pints of Żywiec, play darts, table football or pool and discover what Polish men are really all about... ⓐ Brama Mariacka przy al. Rodła ❶ 055 801 71 01
ⓔ pub@pubbaszta.malbork.pl ❶ 10.00–24.00

Piwniczka £–££ ❷ The Piwniczka is actually contained within the castle walls and can be accessed from the castle or from outside, near the footbridge across the river. There's lots of red-brick vaulting, sturdy wooden benches and tables, stone flooring and a meat-heavy menu fit for a Teutonic knight. Tour bus groups usually head for the Zamek but occasionally invade this place as well. ⓐ ul. Starościńska 1 (in the castle)
❶ 055 273 36 68 ❶ 10.00–24.00

ACCOMMODATION

Hotel Zamek ££ If you desperately must, need or want to stay the night in Malbork (which reverts back to a lifeless provincial backwater once the tourist buses have departed), the Zamek is the best option and nearest to the castle. There is a decent restaurant downstairs. ⓐ ul. Starościńska 14 ❶ 055 272 68 07
ⓦ www.zlotehotele.pl

❶ *Open-air art sale, Gdansk*

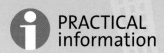

PRACTICAL
information

Directory

GETTING THERE
By air

Three budget airlines operate direct flights from the UK to Gdansk. Ryanair fly in daily from Stansted, Wizz Air from Prestwick, Liverpool and Luton, and Centralwings from Edinburgh. Centralwings also operate flights from Dublin and Shannon, and Wizz Air fly from Cork.

Centralwings Ⓦ www.centralwings.com
LOT Ⓦ www.lot.com
Ryanair Ⓦ www.ryanair.com
Wizz Air Ⓦ www.wizzair.com
Lech Wałęsa Airport Ⓦ www.airport.gdansk.pl ❶ 058 348 11 63

Many people are aware that air travel emits CO_2, which contributes to climate change. You may be interested in the possibility of lessening the environmental impact of your flight through the charity Climate Care, which offsets your CO_2 by

⬤ *SKM commuter trains link the Tri-City area*

funding environmental projects around the world. Visit
Ⓦ www.climatecare.org

By train

PKP run the trains in Poland, and by Western standards the
service is cheap, clean and efficient. Gdansk is well-linked
to the rest of Poland by rail with direct services to and from
Kraków, Poznań, Warsaw, Wrocław and an international
connection to Berlin.

By road

PKS run the buses in Poland. The bus station is situated behind
the railway station. In addition to local and national services,
there are direct coach connections to many cities in Western
Europe, as well as services to Vilnius in Lithuania and the
Russian enclave of Kaliningrad.

By boat

Stena Line and Polferries operate ferries between the
Tri-City and Karlskrona and Nynäshamn in Sweden
respectively.

ENTRY FORMALITIES

Poland is now a fully paid-up member of the EU and should be
part of the Schengen system by 2008; good news for travellers
who like an easy time at borders. Basically, citizens from other
EU countries can stay indefinitely, and those from the US,
Canada, Australia and New Zealand can remain in the country
for a certain length of time (usually 90 days).

MONEY
Currency
The Polish currency is the złoty (pronounced zwo-ti), which is divided into 100 groszy. The abbreviations are zł and gr, though you will very often see PLN used instead of zł. Notes come in denominations of 200zł, 100zł, 50zł, 20zł and 10zł, and there are 5zł, 2zł, 1zł, 50gr, 20gr, 10gr, 5gr, 2gr and 1gr coins.

Credit cards & cheques
Use of credit cards is on the increase but still largely limited to Western businesses, supermarket chains, petrol stations and more upmarket places. Traveller's cheques can be cashed at many banks, but this is a time-consuming process. Credit card fraud is nothing new in Poland, and some of the scams you may have heard about in your own country were possibly devised in this part of Europe, so be on your guard.

Cash machines
There are numerous cash machines accepting foreign cards, though they are not as common as in UK and US cities.

TRAVEL INSURANCE
Travel insurance is always a good idea, and these days a single-trip policy valid for just a couple of days in Europe can cost just a few pounds or dollars. If you are an EU citizen, to access emergency care you will need an EHIC (European Health Insurance Card) which replaced the old E111 in 2004. This is issued free of charge in your home country.

Tax

If you have bought an item in Poland worth more than 200zł, and you are flying out of the EU, you are eligible for a VAT refund.

Changing Currency

For the best rates, change your pounds, dollars and euro at kantors, small booths on street corners, stations etc. You could change your money into złoty before you leave home, or at banks in Poland, but the exchange rates will be worse than at the kantors.

Tipping

Service is included in the bill, but if you are satisfied with the level of service, round up the bill to the nearest 5 or 10 złoty. Taxi drivers don't expect tips, nor do staff at hotels.

HEALTH, SAFETY & CRIME

Health and safety issues have come on in leaps and bounds in recent years. Food hygiene is generally no longer an issue as restaurants and cafés must now comply with EU regulations. Tap water is safe to drink, though it may taste revolting.

Road safety is an issue, and the greatest of care must be taken when crossing the road, never mind when driving along it. If you can use public transport, do so, as few Western drivers will be prepared for Poland's diabolical roads and abysmal drivers.

The standard of health care is good and improving all the time. Private clinics and hospitals may offer a better standard of services than public facilities in the West, but treatment will cost you the arm and leg you've just broken. Paramedic services and facilities are basic by Western standards.

The police are never anywhere to be seen in Poland – that is until you happen to be driving 1 km (half a mile) over the speed limit on a country road at 3am on a Sunday. There are two types of police in Poland – national and municipal.

Despite Eastern Europe's reputation as a crime-ridden place, actual crime rates are, in all likelihood, lower than in your home town. Watch out for pickpockets, bag-snatchers and camera-swipers, especially where large crowds of tourists congregate. Theft from vehicles is common, so don't leave items displayed in your car. At night, stick to well-lit streets and never accept lifts from unofficial taxis.

OPENING HOURS

Shops Open 10.00–18.00 Mon–Fri, 10.00–14.00 Sat
Banks Open 09.00–16.00 Mon–Fri; large city branches 08.00–18.00 Mon–Fri, 09.00–14.00 Sat
Attractions Many close Mondays, otherwise open from around 09.00 or 10.00 until 17.00 or 18.00
Office hours 10.00–18.00 Mon–Fri, 10.00–14.00 Sat

TOILETS

Toalety have improved dramatically in Poland in the last few years, and most are now of a good standard. The only grimy ones you may come across are at railway and bus stations. There can be some confusion among foreigners as to which toilet is for which gender. Just remember that the upside down triangle means 'for men' and the circle 'for women'.

Public toilets are never free so expect to shell out at least 1zł to spend a penny.

CHILDREN

The Tri-City is a relatively child-friendly place, in particular the miles of sandy beaches that line the coast. Malbork Castle can be fun for the little ones, especially if the guide perks up the tour by dressing up in period costume. Taking the kids to see the latest Hollywood blockbuster is also possible, as the films are not dubbed into Polish.

That said, Gdansk is a potential minefield for youngsters. Even the most liberal-minded health and safety officer would have a panic attack on seeing some of the facilities throughout the Tri-City, and this could potentially include kiddies' playgrounds etc. With kids in tow, try to choose restaurants where the little darlings won't form an instant nicotine addiction from passive smoking, and it is imperative that children are supervised near Poland's lethal roads at all times. Baby changing facilities in toilets are almost unheard of.

Here are some ideas for entertaining the kiddies in the Tri-City:

- **Sopot Aquapark** Sopot's modern Aquapark (see page 103) has a variety of pools for all ages and abilities including a year-round outdoor pool and a kiddies' paddling pool.
  ⓐ ul. Zamkowa Góra 3/5 ⓣ 058 555 85 55
  ⓦ www.aquaparksopot.pl ⓔ info@aquaparksopot.pl
  ⓛ 08.00–22.00 Sept–June; 08.30–22.30 July & Aug

- **Oliwa zoo** Kids love zoos, and Gdansk's, with around 1,200 animals, is one of the best in Poland. It's a fair way out of the city centre in the Oliwa district, but you might be in the neighbourhood anyway visiting the cathedral. If you're not, a handy shuttle bus takes you from the tram stop right to the zoo's front gates. **ⓐ** ul. Karwieńska 3 **ⓣ** 058 552 00 42 **ⓦ** www.zoo.gd.pl **ⓔ** zoo@zoo.gd.pl **ⓛ** 09.00–17.00 **ⓝ** Trams: 5,6 and 12 to Oliwa Pętla stop, then change onto shuttle bus 222 **ⓘ** Last entry one hour before closing time

- **Pirate Ship Playground** *Pirates of the Caribbean*-style fun at this playground in the shape of a pirate ship. **ⓐ** Behind Sopot Sailing Club, east of the pier.

COMMUNICATIONS
Telephones
Perhaps due to the relatively low number of mobile phones in Poland, phone boxes seem to stand on every street corner. These are card operated and phonecards are available from newsstands and the post office. The city code must be included when dialling

△ *Distinctive Polish Post box*

a fixed line, meaning all Gdansk numbers start with 058 followed by the seven-digit subscriber number when calling from within Poland. This doesn't apply when calling from mobiles.

Codes

- The country code for Poland is 0048. To ring a number in Gdansk from abroad, dial 0048 58 then the seven digit number.
- To make an international call from Poland, dial 00 then the country code for the country you wish to call, followed by the subscriber number (minus the initial zero).

Post

The post office is run by Poczta Polska and branches are easily recognisable by the yellow post horn symbol somewhere on the outside of the building. Gdansk's main office can be found in the heart of the Main Town ⓐ ul. Długa 23/28 ☎ 058 301 80 49. You'll pay 2.40zł to send a letter or a postcard to another country in Europe and 2.50zł to the USA.

Internet

The number of Wi-fi hotspots is on the increase in central Gdansk with the Café Nescafé, the Alfa Centrum, Daily Café, Soda Café, Salonik and Kamienica cafés.

There are a couple of conveniently located internet cafés in the Main and Old Towns. The imaginatively named **Kawiarnia Internetowa** (Internet Café) ⓐ ul. Karmelicka 1 ☎ 058 320 92 30 🕐 09.00–01.00 is the biggest and most popular, followed by **Spacja** ⓐ ul. Motławska 14 ☎ 058 320 92 30 🕐 11.00–20.00 on Spichlerze Island.

ELECTRICITY

Poland works on 220V AC, 50Hz. To use electrical appliances from home you will need a continental two-pin adaptor.

TRAVELLERS WITH DISABILITIES

Although the situation with access for people with disabilities is improving slowly, it cannot be said that the Tri-City is a particularly wheelchair-friendly environment. Cracked and missing paving stones, cobbles, cars parked on pavements, public transport that is impossible to board and the general danger caused by nutcase drivers on disintegrating roads, are all obstructions to the wheelchair. Some places now have ramps in place, but even the state of these can be woeful. Upmarket hotels have decent facilities for guests, as do some better restaurants. Toilets that are accessible to people with disabilities are being slowly introduced here and there but are very often used by everyone.

DRIVING

Driving in Poland will test your nerve, your car and your patience, and only experienced drivers should even consider it. Driving on the right will be the least of your worries as you negotiate potholes, traffic jams, rude drivers, drunks, speeding, suicidal overtaking and fume-belching Ukrainian trucks, not to mention the overzealous traffic police. The alcohol limit for driving is 0.2 per cent and the fine for exceeding the limit can be up to 500zł. Lights must be used all day from October to April. Where motorways do exist, ridiculously high tolls are charged. The cost of these tolls means many Poles stick to the already crowded and deteriorating minor roads in order to save money.

TOURIST INFORMATION

A swarm of municipal, regional and private agencies publish and distribute tourist information on the Tri-City. It's probably all the same to you no matter who you get the info from.

Tourist information offices are located at:

PTTK ⓐ ul.Długa 45 ❶ 058 301 91 51 Ⓦ www.pttk-gdansk.pl Ⓔ biuro@pttk-gdansk.pl ⓛ 09.00–18.00 daily, May–Sept; 09.00–17.00 Mon–Fri, 09.00–15.00 Sat & Sun Oct–Apr

Gdansk Tourist Information Centre ⓐ ul. Heweliusza 27 ❶ 058 301 43 55 Ⓔ itgdansk@op.pl ⓛ 08.00–18.00 Mon–Fri, May–Sept; 08.00–16.00 Mon–Fri, Oct–Apr

There are also tourist information kiosks at the railway station, the airport and inside the Madison Shopping Centre in the Old Town.

BACKGROUND READING

Possibly the best-known work of literature set in Gdansk is Günter Grass's *The Tin Drum*, which, through the eyes of dwarf Oskar Matzerath, gives an account of life in the pre-war free city of Danzig and the subsequent Nazi occupation of the city. Grass was born in Danzig, though later moved to West Germany. He caused controversy in both Germany and Poland in 2006 by revealing he had been a member of the SS during World War II.

Veritable mines of information on the Tri-City are the expat Gdansk-life.com and the *Gdansk In Your Pocket* guide handed out by tourist offices.

Emergencies

EMERGENCY NUMBERS

Poland doesn't have one general number for the emergency services, but a different one for each (see below). The ambulance number is easy for Brits to remember as it's 999. Though many may not be aware of the fact, dialling 112 from a mobile in any country in the EU should get you through to the emergency services, but this cannot be entirely relied upon. The above numbers are for real emergencies only, not for asking directions to the nearest cash machine and alike (it happens!).

Ambulance: 999   **Police**: 997

City Police: 986   **Fire**: 998

MEDICAL SERVICES

The main public hospital in Gdansk is the **County Hospital** just to the west of the Main Town ⓐ Nowe Ogrody 1/6 ⓣ 058 302 30 31

H Centrum Stomatologiczne is one of the best places to contact for dental help ⓐ ul. Miszewskiego 12/13 ⓣ 058 341 59 41 ⓦ www.hcentrum.pl

Medicover is open 24 hours a day ⓐ ul. Beniowskiego 23 ⓣ 058 557 55 55 ⓦ www.medicover.com

Swissmed is a recently built private clinic and hospital where English is spoken ⓐ ul. Wileńska 44 ⓣ 058 524 15 00 ⓦ www.swissmed.com.pl

ROADSIDE ASSISTANCE

Calling the number 96 37 anywhere in Poland will get you through to the nearest **PZM** (Polish Motoring Association) service centre ⓦ www.pzm.pl

EMBASSIES & CONSULATES

The UK is the only English-speaking country to have an honorary consul in Gdansk. Americans, Australians and New Zealanders must contact their embassies in distant Warsaw.
ⓐ ul. Grunwaldzka 102 ⓣ 058 341 43 65 ⓔ consul@abcc.com.pl
ⓛ 09.00–15.00 Mon–Fri.

EMERGENCY PHRASES

Help!	Pomocy!	*Po-mo-ste!*
Fire!	Pożar!	*Po-jar!*
Stop!	Stop!	*Stop!*
Call an ambulance/ a doctor/ the police/ the fire service!	Wezwać pogotowie/ lekarza/ policję/ straż pożarna!	*Ve-zvach po-go-toh-vyeh/ le-ka-jah/ po-lee-tsyeh straj po-jar-nom!*

The publishers would like to thank the following individuals and organisations for providing their copyright photos for this book.

Marc Di Duca: all except: Fotolia: page 11 (Namq), page 47 (Bartlomiej Kwieciszewski), page 91 (Jerzy Czarkowski); Hotel Podewils: page 39; Sco: pages 23, 34, 85, 113; Visit Poland: pages 6, 15, 21, 25, 32, 36, 59, 67, 99, 103, 121, 127; World Pictures: page 19

Copy editor: Jenni Rainford
Proofreader: Ali Rasch

Send your thoughts to
books@thomascook.com

- **Found a great bar, club, shop or must-see sight that we don't feature?**
- **Like to tip us off about any information that needs updating?**
- **Want to tell us what you love about this handy little guidebook and more importantly how we can make it even handier?**

Then here's your chance to tell all! Send us ideas, discoveries and recommendations today and then look out for your valuable input in the next edition of this title. As an extra 'thank you' from Thomas Cook Publishing, you'll be automatically entered into our exciting prize draw.

Send an email to the above address (stating the book's title) or write to:
CitySpots Project Editor, Thomas Cook Publishing, PO Box 227,
The Thomas Cook Business Park, Unit 18, Coningsby Road,
Peterborough PE3 8SB, UK.